O9-BHK-701

Sky Soldiers

LEE COUNTY LIBRARY
107 HAWKINS AVE.
SANFORD, N. C. 27330

Carrying ground troops across the rugged wastes of Fort Irwin, California, UH-60 Black Hawk helicopters of the 101st Airborne Division (Air Assault) fly in trail formation.

Troops of the 101st Airborne sprint from UH-60s landing in Iraq at the start of the
Desert Storm ground campaign. In the largest air assault ever, more than 300 Black
Hawks and other helicopters sped 3,000 men and tons of artillery, fuel, and ammunition
fifty miles into enemy territory on the first day of fighting.

Giving proof that the helicopter can deliver ground forces to any kind of terrain—swamp, jungle, or mountains—troops rappel from a hovering Black Hawk.

Tandem-rotor CH-47D Chinooks airlift heavy equipment to clear a landing zone. With twin 3,750-hp engines, the D model can lift as much as 35,000 pounds, four times as much as its Vietnam-era predecessors.

Looking before it leaps upward from the concealment of trees, an OH-58D Kiowa scout checks the terrain ahead with television and infrared eyes mounted above the rotor.

Delivering a deadly sting, an AH-64 Apache attack helicopter pours a stream of 70-mm rockets toward a target. The gunship's armament also includes a 30-mm cannon and missiles that can hit a tank miles away.

Other Publications:

HOW THINGS WORK
WINGS OF WAR
CREATIVE EVERYDAY COOKING
COLLECTOR'S LIBRARY OF THE UNKNOWN
CLASSICS OF WORLD WAR II
TIME-LIFE LIBRARY OF CURIOUS AND UNUSUAL FACTS
AMERICAN COUNTRY
VOYAGE THROUGH THE UNIVERSE
THE THIRD REICH
THE TIME-LIFE GARDENER'S GUIDE
MYSTERIES OF THE UNKNOWN
TIME FRAME
FIX IT YOURSELF
FITNESS, HEALTH & NUTRITION
SUCCESSFUL PARENTING
HEALTHY HOME COOKING
UNDERSTANDING COMPUTERS
LIBRARY OF NATIONS
THE ENCHANTED WORLD
THE KODAK LIBRARY OF CREATIVE PHOTOGRAPHY
GREAT MEALS IN MINUTES
THE CIVIL WAR
PLANET EARTH
COLLECTOR'S LIBRARY OF THE CIVIL WAR
THE EPIC OF FLIGHT
THE GOOD COOK
WORLD WAR II
HOME REPAIR AND IMPROVEMENT
THE OLD WEST

For information on and a full description of
any of the Time-Life Books series listed above,
please call 1-800-621-7026 or write:
Reader Information
Time-Life Customer Service
P.O. Box C-32068
Richmond, Virginia 23261-2068

THE NEW FACE OF WAR

Sky Soldiers

BY THE EDITORS OF
TIME-LIFE BOOKS, ALEXANDRIA, VIRGINIA

CONSULTANTS

MAJOR COLIN S. CONNOR commanded the Reconnaissance Platoon of Great Britain's Parachute Regiment, Second Battalion (Two Para), in the 1982 Falklands war.

JOHN S. DUVALL is the director of the 82d Airborne Division War Memorial Museum at Fort Bragg, North Carolina. A historian of airborne infantry, he was trained at Kenyon College and the University of North Carolina at Chapel Hill. He also served as a logistician with the U.S. Air Force from 1961 to 1968.

COLONEL DAVID M. GLANTZ, director and chief of research at the U.S. Army's Soviet Army Studies Office, currently is working on a history of Soviet military strategy. He has written many articles and books about Soviet military affairs.

COLONEL JOHN R. HOCKER (Ret.) served as special assistant to the Supreme Allied Commander Europe and is a former battalion commander in the 82d Airborne Division. He helped to train Khmer Army parachute and special-missions units and served in the First Cavalry Division (Airmobile) in Vietnam.

DAVID C. ISBY, a Washington-based attorney and consultant on national security matters, has written widely on the Soviet military. In studying the war in Afghanistan, he traveled with the Afghan resistance in the early 1980s.

GENERAL HARRY W. O. KINNARD served with the 101st Airborne Division in World War II and had key responsibility in developing the airmobile concept as commander of both the 11th Airborne Assault Test Division and the First Cavalry Division (Airmobile) in Vietnam.

GENERAL JAMES J. LINDSAY, former Commander in Chief, U.S. Special Operations Command, held nine different assignments with the 82d Airborne Division, from platoon leader to division commander. Recently retired from active duty, he is the president of the Airborne-Special Operations Museum Foundation, Inc.

LIEUTENANT GENERAL HAROLD G. MOORE commanded the First Battalion, Seventh Cavalry Regiment, of the First Cavalry (Airmobile) in Vietnam. In 1965, he led his troops to battle in the Ia Drang Valley, the first use of U.S. airmobile forces. Now retired from the Army, he is writing a book about the experience.

LIEUTENANT COLONEL CHARLES R. SHRADER, a military historian since his retirement, has more than twenty years' experience in the Army as an officer in the infantry and the transportation corps.

VLADISLAV TAMAROV, a freelance photographer who lives in Leningrad, served with the Soviet airborne in Afghanistan clearing mines. His pictures from the war have appeared in a variety of publications and have been sold to private collectors. Tamarov is currently working on a book about the war in Afghanistan.

CONTENTS

"This Aggression Will Not Stand!"

Just days after the Iraqi invasion of Kuwait in August 1990, paratroopers of the U.S. 82d Airborne Division—the leading edge of Operation Desert Shield—disembark from a C5A military transport at an air base in Saudi Arabia. The division is kept ready for immediate deployment in a crisis.

Nations sometimes flex their military muscles simply to intimidate, and to most observers, the buildup of Iraqi arms along the border with Kuwait in the summer of 1990 appeared to be just such a display—this one aimed, among other things, at cowing the tiny, oil-rich sheikdom into forgiving billions of dollars in debt incurred during Iraq's recently ended eight-year war with Iran.

On August 2, however, Iraq's dictator, Saddam Hussein, attacked. In a matter of days, his armor and infantry rolled across Kuwait and began to dig in along Kuwait's border with Saudi Arabia to the south. Perhaps the Iraqis were merely taking up positions to defend their victory, but a military threat must first be assessed according to an opponent's capabilities, not his intentions. Iraq surely had the means to shrug aside the hopelessly frail forces of Saudi Arabia and grab control of the bulk of the world's oil.

Thus four days later, at the request of the legitimate Kuwaiti government and the endangered Saudi Arabians, President George Bush ordered U.S. military intervention on the Arabian Peninsula. The action was named Operation Desert Shield, and immediately, three U.S. Navy aircraft carrier battle groups headed at flank speed for positions in the Red Sea and the northern Arabian Sea. Scores, then hundreds of Air Force tactical fighters and bombers deployed to Saudi airfields from bases in the United States. And within hours of the president's decision, the vanguard of the U.S. Army's famed 82d Airborne Division prepared to emplane for Saudi Arabia.

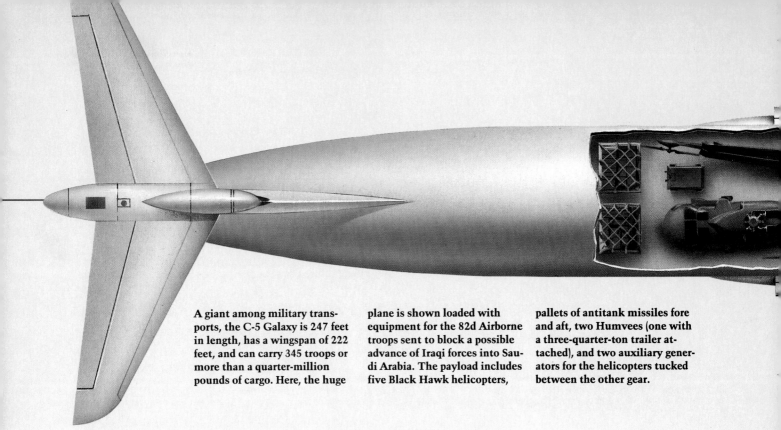

A giant among military transports, the C-5 Galaxy is 247 feet in length, has a wingspan of 222 feet, and can carry 345 troops or more than a quarter-million pounds of cargo. Here, the huge plane is shown loaded with equipment for the 82d Airborne troops sent to block a possible advance of Iraqi forces into Saudi Arabia. The payload includes five Black Hawk helicopters, pallets of antitank missiles fore and aft, two Humvees (one with a three-quarter-ton trailer attached), and two auxiliary generators for the helicopters tucked between the other gear.

Neither air power nor the lightly armed sky soldiers of the 82d would be sufficient in themselves to halt an Iraqi army of 1,000,000 soldiers, 5,500 tanks, and 3,700 artillery pieces supplied largely by the Soviets. But sending men and women of the United States' armed services, particularly ground forces, was a "line drawn in the sand," as George Bush told the nation—a clear signal of American resolve. To conquer Saudi Arabia, Saddam Hussein would have to go through the 82d. And while the Iraqis pondered the consequences of that act, the United States and its allies began gathering the heavy forces needed to expel the aggressors from Kuwait.

Once the decision to send American troops to the Persian Gulf was made, the choice of the 82d was inevitable. Along with a number of Marine expeditionary brigades, the 82d is the nation's quick-reaction ground force, ready to respond within eighteen hours to crises anywhere in the world and to sustain itself without reinforcement for seventy-two hours after arriving. One of the division's three brigades is always on alert, serving a six-week tour as the division ready brigade (DRB) at the 82d's sprawling Fort Bragg base near Fayetteville, North Carolina. Standing by as well are 105-mm howitzers and rapid-fire Vulcan air defense cannons, Sheridan light tanks mounting 152-mm guns, HMMVV utility vehicles—called Humvees or Hummers—equipped with TOW antitank missile launchers, plus troop-carrying Black Hawk and tank-killing Apache helicopters. As one airborne officer put it: "When you send the 82d, people know you mean business."

Desert Shield began for the 82d Airborne Division and its DRB—

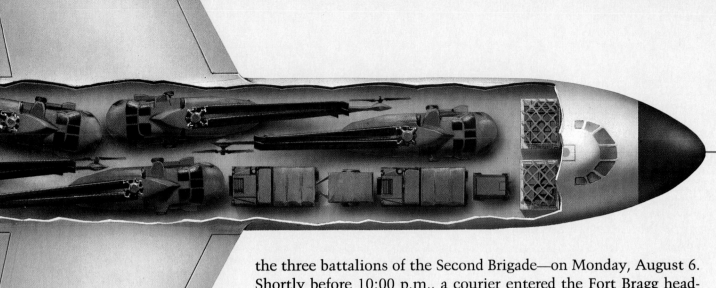

the three battalions of the Second Brigade—on Monday, August 6. Shortly before 10:00 p.m., a courier entered the Fort Bragg headquarters of XVIII Airborne Corps, the 82d's parent organization, opened a sealed briefcase, and handed the duty officer a message that began: "This is an execute order by authority and direction of the secretary of defense."

The officer hurried downstairs to the emergency operations center and picked up a "red line" telephone. Without dialing, he was instantly connected to the command center of the 82d Airborne by way of an encrypted circuit. Within minutes, telephones began ringing as soldiers of the Second were recalled to Fort Bragg from every corner of Fayetteville—and from wherever else they happened to be. N-hour (notification hour) had arrived, and the clock was ticking toward N+18, when the first transports laden with the 82d's ready brigade were scheduled to lift off from Pope Air Force Base, adjacent to Fort Bragg.

During the intervening hours, nearly 300 separate procedures and actions were carried out according to an intricate, highly orchestrated timetable. By N+2, for example, almost all the troopers of the Second's lead battalion, designated as Division Ready Force One, had arrived at the assembly area; the men were now isolated with MPs posted to guard against potential terrorists and to keep the news media at bay. The Second's two other battalions had been alerted; standing plans called for them to enter the eighteen-hour sequence at six-hour intervals.

At N+2 also, the Second's officers received a briefing that outlined a multifold mission. Besides acting as a deterrent, the brigade was to secure the big Saudi air base at Dhahran and the nearby port at Al Jubayl Naval Base for the arrival of forces sufficient to defeat an Iraqi invasion. Meanwhile, the Second would operate from two vacant compounds, including one near the Kuwaiti border owned by the Arabian American Oil Company.

By now, all officers on detached duty or otherwise off-base had been recalled to Fort Bragg to join in detailed planning. Lieutenant Colonel David Abrahamson, scheduled to take command of one of

the brigade's battalions, was on an exercise at Fort Chaffee, Arkansas. When word arrived, he rushed back to Fayetteville and plunged into the work. Major Mike Molosso, a vacationing but critically important personnel officer, was having a beer at Crescent Beach, Florida, when the call came; he drove all night and was back in Fayetteville by 10 a.m. Tuesday. By then, the 82d's two other brigades were gearing up for Operation Desert Shield. One entire battalion of the First Brigade was away on block leave, but its commander, Lieutenant Colonel Harry Axson, and his staff had 90 percent of the soldiers on post within eight hours.

Meanwhile, the Second Brigade's Ready Force One began inspecting its equipment and moving it to the Green Ramp, an aircraft-loading area on Pope Air Force Base. A convoy of trucks hauled ammunition. The first twenty-nine of the Sheridans and other vehicles to be taken along by Ready One rumbled toward their rendezvous with the Air Force. Mechanics started preparing helicopters for loading into C-5 Galaxies when the aircraft arrived. Black Hawks had their rotor blades folded; Apaches had them removed.

All this was strictly according to a script called RSOP, for readiness standard operating procedure. Yet as the hands of the clock moved inexorably toward N+18, details were tailored to suit the specific requirements of Operation Desert Shield. From supply depots in Philadelphia and elsewhere came truckloads of beige-and-brown desert camouflage suits, 15,000 in all; from the Defense Mapping Agency in suburban Washington came a deluge of tactical maps; and to help defend against Iraqi tanks, the 82d called on a battalion of field artillery from XVIII Airborne Corps for a trio of MLRSs (multiple-launch rocket systems) and crews to man them. Each of the nearly 100 rockets supplied for these weapons could carry a warhead of tank-killing bomblets nearly nineteen miles, against eleven miles for the division's own 105-mm howitzers.

To combat the Arabian heat, each man was issued a five-quart bladder in addition to the usual one- and two-quart containers. For protection against the sun, goggles, tinted glasses, sunscreen, and lip balm were provided. Most ominously—and in grim recognition of Iraq's oft-demonstrated willingness to use chemical weapons—each man was outfitted with protective equipment as well as syringes filled with atropine, an antidote for nerve agents.

By noon on August 7—four hours ahead of schedule—the Second's Ready Force One was set to go. The men waited in the mar-

The Chemical and Biological Threat

Four paratroops from the 82d Airborne Division train in Saudi Arabia wearing chemical-warfare garb. To drink without removing his headgear (inset), a soldier uses a special tube passed from his canteen through an airtight opening in the mask. Wrapped around the trooper's upraised arm is a paper strip that turns red upon contact with droplets of blister or nerve agents.

Short of nuclear arms, no weapons evoke more fear than chemical and biological agents. Easy to spread by land mines, aircraft, rockets, or artillery, such weapons can be delivered virtually anywhere on the battlefield. Some chemicals, called nerve agents because of their effect on the human nervous system, are so lethal that one drop can kill in half a minute. Other chemicals last so long after dispersal they can turn whole battlefields into toxic no man's lands. Lewisite and mustard, two liquids that blister the skin and lungs and inflame the eyes, and VX, a nerve agent in the United States arsenal of chemical weapons, can be effective not just for days but for weeks. Biological weapons are no less fearsome: The hardy spores that cause anthrax, a deadly respiratory disease, can remain viable for years.

The first use of poisonous gases and biological weapons such as anthrax has been banned by international agreement, but American soldiers go to war ready for both—just in case. To survive an attack, early warning is crucial. Unfortunately, biological weapons can be recognized for certain only by the symptoms they cause in their victims. But chemical agents can be detected in minuscule concentrations by a number of high-tech tools, including the Fox, an armored reconnaissance vehicle that functions as a laboratory on wheels. Using an instrument called a mass spectrometer and computers, specially trained teams are able to analyze air and soil samples from forward areas, to determine the location and type of any chemical hazard. Troops farther from the front rely on less complicated battery-powered devices that either sound alarms or flash lights when sensors pick up traces of the odorless nerve agents. Forewarned, the soldiers should have enough time to don protective hooded masks and two-piece charcoal-lined MOPP suits that guard against both chemical and biological weapons.

23

shaling area while the Military Airlift Command's Starlifters and Galaxies sped critical command, control, and maintenance systems to Air Force fighter units already dispatched to Saudi bases. More time was needed to transport the 82d's vanguard to the desert. Altogether, nineteen more hours passed before the first elements of the 82d's ready brigade were wheels up at N+39, heading east in MAC transports and civilian jetliners that had been commandeered for the occasion.

After a flight of seventeen tense, tiring hours punctuated by two stops to refuel, the first troopers of the 82d Airborne landed in Saudi Arabia and filed from the planes at Dhahran in fighting humor and full combat array—their faces smeared with camouflage grease paint, M16 rifles at the ready.

That the 82d was welcomed by American and Saudi liaison officers instead of waves of attacking Iraqis might make the aggressive demeanor of the arriving troops seem a trifle comical to outsiders. (The flight attendants on the airliners were particularly amused.) But the airborne mission is to land prepared for a fight. And though Dhahran was in friendly hands at N+56 when the troops arrived, no one knew what might lie ahead in the next few hours and days. Within six weeks, all three brigades of the 82d plus supporting artillery, helicopter, and light tank units, 15,000 troopers all told, were in Saudi Arabia. Later, the First Marine Expeditionary Brigade, with 16,500 men, began to arrive in Saudi Arabia from California. More Marines followed.

As these lightly armed forces prepared to fight, they worried that Saddam Hussein would send his multitudes south against them

About forty miles inside Iraq, troops of the 82d Airborne Division's Second Brigade search three of the thousands of Iraqis they took prisoner in the first days of the Desert Storm ground war. Moving by land, the paratroops quickly secured a two-lane highway that would serve as a main supply route for coalition forces sweeping northward to outflank Iraqi divisions occupying Kuwait.

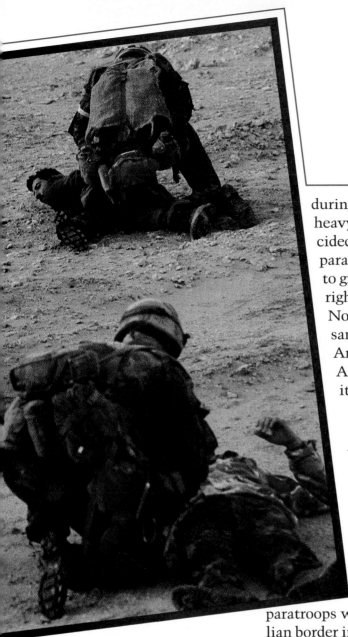

during the three weeks or so that would pass before U.S. heavy armor could arrive to back them up. "If Hussein decided to come across the border," said one of the earliest 82d paratroopers to arrive, "the Second Brigade would be there to grease the treads of all those tanks, 'cause they would go right over the top of us."

No attack came. Thin though President Bush's line in the sand may have been, the Iraqi Army chose not to cross it. And six months later, the 82d, side by side with the 101st Airborne, would lance deeply into southern Iraq, doing its part to vanquish Saddam Hussein's mammoth army.

Almost unnoticed in the dramatic move of the paratroops to Saudi Arabia was the fact that they had left most of their parachutes at Fort Bragg. Yet that apparent anomaly reflected more than a half-century of evolution in the concept of assault from the air.

The idea was pioneered by the Soviet Union. In 1935, the Red Army staged a massive exercise in which 1,500 men parachuted from dozens of aircraft that had taken off from a base 175 miles distant. Soviet paratroops walked into action against the Japanese on the Mongolian border in 1939 and against the Finns in the short, brutal Russo-Finnish War that same year.

A keen observer of Soviet efforts was Germany's General Kurt Student, who formed an airborne division for the assault of Hitler's Wehrmacht on France and the Low Countries. On May 10, 1940, the general stunned the world by sending fewer than 400 of these troops—some by parachute, others in gliders—to capture the bridges over Belgium's Albert Canal and overcome the 1,200-man garrison at Fort Eben Emael. In doing so, Student opened the way for a German thrust into Holland, Belgium, and France. A year later, German paratroops won fame again in the conquest of Greece. By cutting off the Allied retreat toward Crete and ultimately Egypt, Hitler's airborne forces made possible the capture of thousands of British and Greek troops who might otherwise have regrouped to fight again.

Very little seemed beyond Student's "hunters from the skies," and for his next triumph, the paratroop general planned to capture

Crete, a rugged island fortress held by 30,000 troops of the British Commonwealth plus 10,000 Greek and Cretan irregulars. He planned to commit his entire 9,500-man Seventh Airborne Division along with the Fifth Mountain Division and other troops. In a lightning campaign, they intended to validate, beyond doubt, the strategy of airborne invasion.

The Germans succeeded in taking Crete, but it was a Pyrrhic victory, a bloodletting that for the first time defined the limitations of paratroops. Heretofore, they had always achieved tactical surprise, and always, they had been reinforced within hours by a breakthrough of heavy panzer divisions. Now, in the assault on Crete, they were alone, lightly armed, and without benefit of surprise against a numerous, well-dug-in, and determined enemy. Waves of Junkers transports lumbered confidently overhead in broad daylight and released their sticks of paratroopers directly above Allied positions. The cream of the German airborne were first decimated in their parachutes and then slaughtered on the ground as they struggled to form into units. Only raw courage and superb training enabled them to rally and seize an airstrip on which the Fifth Mountain Division could land with artillery and fresh supplies. In the end, the German paratroopers paid the ghastly price of 42 percent casualties, including 4,000 killed, and 170 of 500 transport aircraft were shot down. Hitler himself was appalled at the losses. Never again would he permit a major airborne operation. Crete, lamented Student, "was the graveyard of the German parachutists."

Still, the early German successes had a profound effect on Allied military planners, and on June 25, 1940—three days after France surrendered to Germany—the U.S. Army authorized an experimental parachute platoon to consist of one officer and forty-eight enlisted men at Fort Benning, Georgia. In its call for volunteers, the Army issued a chilling warning: The project, it said, "will require frequent jumps from airplanes, which may result in serious injury or death, therefore, only unmarried men may volunteer." Two hundred did so, and on August 16, Lieutenant William T. Ryder stepped out of an Army Air Corps C-33 transport flying 1,500 feet over Georgia to become the first U.S. paratrooper.

During the war, the U.S. airborne force grew to five divisions and several independent parachute regiments and battalions that made nineteen combat jumps and glider assaults behind enemy lines in the Philippines, the North African desert, the hills and plains of

Sicily, the hedgerows of Normandy, and the Dutch lowlands. More often than not, the airborne units suffered heavy casualties after landing, and were sometimes scattered across the landscape and sometimes unable to hold off the enemy until stronger forces could break through to them.

Hazards of dropping from the sky notwithstanding, even the parachutists' harshest critics agreed that they were superlative soldiers—carefully selected, rigorously trained, bonded by the shared experience of jumping from airplanes, and to a degree often viewed as arrogance, deeply imbued with a sense of their own special nature. In times of high crisis, these formidable warriors might be more successful if they did not have to jump into battle.

Thus the tough troopers of Germany's First Parachute Division clambered afoot up precipitous slopes to bulwark the bitter defense of Monte Cassino. On the Eastern Front, tens of thousands of Soviet airborne troops contributed to the defense of Kiev but failed to keep the Wehrmacht at bay. And in northern France, the Americans of the 82d and 101st airborne divisions were rushed by truck from reserve to help stop advancing Germans in the near-disastrous Battle of the Bulge.

After the war, Britain disbanded its two parachute divisions, eventually reducing itself to a single parachute regiment—and then would call upon its two battalions to win back the Falkland Islands from Argentine invaders. The Soviets, never ones to cut back on numbers, built the world's largest and most heavily equipped airborne apparatus, and would employ it with increasing urgency in the debilitating struggle against Mujahedin guerrillas in Afghanistan. America deactivated three of its five wartime parachute divisions, but retained the 82d and the Eleventh. After serving as the occupation force in Japan, the Eleventh Division would be deactivated in 1958. But the 82d, along with the newly reactivated 101st Airborne Division, would fight with distinction in the long, frustrating struggle over Vietnam. In Panama, America's 82d Airborne would help to oust a malevolent dictator just eight months before responding to the Persian Gulf crisis.

And along the way, advancing technology would give the sky soldiers new weapons and a means of transport—the helicopter—that would revolutionize the airborne mission.   ★

2

Winged Mounts for the U.S. Cavalry

Launching a search-and-destroy operation in July 1967, a UH-1D Huey delivers troops of the U.S. First Cavalry Division to a rocky ridge in the Buc Pho area of South Vietnam. By their mastery of the country's difficult terrain—mostly mountain, jungle, or wetland—helicopters became an indispensable adjunct to the ground war in Vietnam.

No fanfare attended the arrival of the U.S. escort carrier *Card* in Saigon on December 11, 1961. A war was on, and America was in it—but only in a small way. Ostensibly, the sole U.S. military role was to advise and help train the Army of the Republic of Vietnam (ARVN) in its struggle against Communist insurgents. The *Card*, however, heralded a significant reshaping of that low profile. Strapped to the carrier's deck were thirty-two U.S. Army Shawnee helicopters—big, dual-rotor craft well suited to carrying troops into battle. These particular choppers would be piloted by Americans, demonstrating a newfound American willingness to aid South Vietnam in combat operations, particularly with aviation support.

That first modest inclination would, in the space of a few years, grow into an enormous national commitment. Ahead lay an ultimately fruitless ordeal that would bring nearly nine million U.S. soldiers to this tropical land and would claim nearly 58,000 American lives. It would be a war unlike any other ever fought by the United States, lacking conventional battle lines, waged mostly by small actions against an elusive enemy, shaped by political considerations that restrained the full use of American power. At times, it would have an almost phantasmagoric fluidity, characterized by rapid shifting of men and weaponry across sodden lowlands, jungle-clad mountains, and lush valleys—insertions and extractions of troops in response to a jack-in-the-box enemy. The prime agent of all that movement would be rotary-wing aircraft, first seen in the form of the ungainly deck cargo of the *Card*. Vietnam would become known as the Helicopter War—and the Shawnees soon showed why.

Less than two weeks after their arrival, thirty of the helicopters—giant green flying bananas—rose from Saigon's Tan Son Nhut Airport and formed up in a ragged line. At the controls were U.S. Army pilots of the 57th Transportation Detachment (Light Helicopter). The Shawnees fluttered west over a verdant landscape of fields and rice paddies, heading for a village about ten miles from Saigon. The hamlet, sited along a tree-lined canal, was believed to be the headquarters of a Vietcong rifle company that guarded a clandestine radio transmitter. A dozen combat-ready ARVN paratroopers rode in the belly of each chopper, ready to take the guerrillas on. The helicopters themselves were unarmed; it was hoped that the VC would not fire on them for fear of provoking American wrath.

Within minutes, the Shawnees descended toward their target, splitting into two groups as they approached. They flared sharply to cut their airspeed and stopped in a hover inches above pineapple fields on either side of the canal. The ARVN paratroopers jumped out and ran toward the canal, firing as they advanced. The Vietcong fired back from the cover of a line of trees. Some of their shots seemed directed at the Shawnees, dispelling any notions of American immunity. Immediately, all but one of the helicopters leaped away. That one was in trouble, the pilot having somehow planted a wheel in mud at the edge of the landing zone. Roaring as it struggled to pull free, the Shawnee spun around on the mired wheel, then toppled over, crushing one ARVN soldier to death and seriously injuring another. The Americans climbed out of the wrecked chopper and waited close by. Soon, another Shawnee swooped down and lifted them to safety, along with the injured soldier.

The men of the 57th never discovered the outcome of the engagement, but the value of the Shawnees was crystal-clear. By taking an air route to battle, the helicopters had drastically reduced travel time, gained the advantage of surprise, and negated the all-too-familiar dangers of a mined road or an ambush on the ground. They had also pulled men out of trouble in a hurry. But their demonstrated usefulness for troop transport was the merest foretaste of what helicopters would mean in Vietnam. In the months and years to come, rotary-wing aircraft of various kinds would play a multitude of other roles: They would be used for reconnaissance (often locating the enemy by intentionally drawing fire); they would deliver ammunition, food, water, and other supplies to the scene of fighting, no matter what the terrain; they would lift artillery batteries across the landscape; they would function as airborne observation and command posts in battle; they would taxi commanders and officials to remote locales; they would save countless lives by swift evacuation of the wounded; they would rescue downed aviators from the clutches of the enemy—and would also pluck damaged helicopters from the jungle so that they could be repaired. Most visibly of all, they would become formidable weapons platforms—gunships—that could complement or supplant fixed-wing aircraft in providing ground troops with close air support.

All of these roles and others would be summed up in the term *airmobility*, a concept whose features were just taking shape in 1961. At that time, some military planners saw the helicopter as catalyzing a revolution; others believed that these relatively slow-moving craft would fare poorly in the rigors of war. The fighting in Vietnam would be the acid test.

In 1920, a Spanish aristocrat and aviation enthusiast named Juan de la Cierva hit upon a new way to fly. He realized that if a free-turning rotor was set spinning and at the same time was moved forward through the air, it would continue to spin and would generate lift just like the fixed wing of an airplane. Moreover, an aircraft utilizing this principle would be able to stay aloft while traveling far more slowly than an airplane—as little as twenty miles per hour. And if the forward motion ceased, the aircraft would descend safely to earth as its windmilling rotor slowed the drop.

After considerable trial and error, la Cierva translated his idea into a remarkable craft that performed exactly as he had hoped. Called the autogiro, it was, in essence, a wingless airplane with a single big rotor mounted atop the fuselage and a standard airplane engine and propeller to provide the forward motion that kept the rotor turning. La Cierva himself flew his creation across the English Channel in 1928. The aviation industry, agog at the marvel, began building autogiros by the score. One American entrepreneur offered a so-called sports version for $5,000. It was his expectation that the autogiro, capable of speeds up to 100 miles per hour and needing little room to take off or land, would be the Model T of the air.

The public did not agree, but at least the autogiro generated a good deal of military interest. The Italian Navy tested it in a reconnaissance role, and the Japanese actually put the craft into service in 1944, flying autogiros from the escort carrier *Akitsu Maru* on antisubmarine patrols. But by then, engineering work on la Cierva's

31

invention had shown the way toward the true helicopter, fitted with an engine-driven rotor. Its great advantage was the ability to rise vertically, something the autogiro could do only in a strong headwind. Within a few years, the autogiro had been completely eclipsed by this new form of powered flight.

Helicopter design advanced most swiftly in Germany. The year 1940 saw the introduction of the world's first completely viable helicopter, the Fl-282 Kolbri, or Hummingbird. Fitted, eggbeater-fashion, with a pair of counterrotating rotors, the machine could climb to 13,000 feet and travel at nearly ninety miles per hour. Tests showed that a pilot could land the craft on the flat top of a cruiser gun turret, even in heavy seas. The German Navy ordered 1,000 of the Hummingbirds.

The U.S. military favored single-rotor helicopters, a design pioneered by a gifted Russian émigré, Igor Sikorsky. In April 1944, one such craft inaugurated a new role for helicopters—medical evacuation: A Sikorsky R-4 was sent behind enemy lines in Burma to rescue an American pilot and three British casualties who had gone down in the jungle in an airplane. The R-4 landed safely in a small jungle clearing but had a harder time getting out. Because of the altitude, humidity, and high air temperature, the R-4 generated so little lift at full power that the men had to be taken out one at a time.

Medevac would be carried out on a grand scale during the Korean War. Bubble-nosed Bell 47 helicopters flying in support of the four

In a pioneering air assault staged on November 6, 1956, British Whirlwind helicopters land Royal Marines at Port Said in response to Egypt's attempt to wrest the Suez Canal from Anglo-French control. In less than two hours, choppers flying from a carrier ten miles offshore delivered 415 men and twenty-five tons of supplies to the bridgehead.

mobile army surgical hospitals (MASHes) in Korea evacuated about 30,000 casualties during the war; many lives were saved by getting wounded men to a hospital within an hour instead of the ten to fourteen hours that ambulances typically needed to lurch across the rugged Korean terrain.

Watching the nimble choppers skim over the ridges and mountains, landing wherever they pleased, regimental and battalion commanders adopted helicopters for their own use. But lifesaving duties and a command-and-control role were just the beginning of the story of rotary-wing aircraft in Korea. Another application was launched during the rainy week of September 13, 1951. At that time, fighting had stagnated into trench warfare along the thirty-eighth parallel, broken by bitter skirmishes for such high ground as Heartbreak Ridge and Porkchop Hill. When the Second Battalion, First Marines, clawed its way up the gluey sides of Hill 673 against stiff resistance by North Korean and Chinese Communist troops, a swarm of HRS-1 helicopters—muscular Sikorskys that could lift 2,000 pounds—appeared in the skies. They dropped a day's supplies to the beleaguered troops, then took out the wounded.

Less than a week later, the airlift concept was expanded when Marine choppers delivered 224 troops and almost 18,000 pounds of supplies onto Hill 884 to relieve a hard-hit South Korean unit. It was the first time troops had been helitransported into combat. By the end of that year, 2,000 men and seventy-five tons of supplies were being lifted each month, and during a five-day period in 1953—the last year of the war—Marine copters airlifted 800 tons of supplies.

Meanwhile, other nations were pursuing the military potential of rotary-wing craft. The French used about a dozen helicopters—primarily for medevac—in their losing battle to hold on to their colony of Indochina in the early 1950s, and the British used the machines for reconnaissance and troop insertions, and sometimes as gunships against hidden guerrillas in their successful counterinsurgency efforts in Malaya. In 1956, Britain and France joined forces to regain control of the Suez Canal after it had been seized by Egypt. On November 6, twenty-two helicopters filled with British

Royal Marines lifted off from two aircraft carriers and flew ten miles to Port Said, establishing a toehold for other Marines who would later land there. This operation was the first helicopter assault under fire—although the opposition was so light that it did not amount to a real test.

The next step in the evolution of military helicopters was taken by the French in their eight-year fight to retain yet another colony, Algeria. Into this guerrilla war, France introduced the Sud-Est Alouette II, or Horned Butterfly, a four-passenger, single-rotor craft embodying important advances. Instead of the conventional gasoline engine, it had a type of jet engine known as a turboshaft. This power plant was a marked improvement over its piston predecessors. With fewer moving parts, it was more reliable. It could produce three times as much power as a piston engine of equal weight and was small enough to mount on top of the helicopter. It ran more smoothly, was self-cooling, burned cheap kerosene rather than aviation fuel, and used less fuel while hovering to load or unload troops. The turboshaft quickly became standard on helicopters.

The French used the Horned Butterfly primarily for reconnaissance, but a few of the helicopters were armed with machine guns, rockets, and even antitank missiles. While transport choppers were putting down troops in a hot landing zone, these early gunships could protect them with a tempest of suppressive fire.

The Algerian guerrillas found some ways of countering this new tool of war. They mined or booby-trapped potential landing zones. They dug trenches, tunnels, and other forms of shelter against attacks. They learned to mortar the birds when they touched down or to blaze away at them in the skies with small arms and machine-gun fire. By the time of the cease-fire in 1962, the rebels had downed dozens of the 600 helicopters the French sent into the conflict.

In the United States a few years earlier, some improvised experiments with the helicopter as a weapons platform had been conducted at the Army Aviation School at Fort Rucker, Alabama, by a resourceful staff officer, Colonel Jay Vanderpool. In 1956 and 1957, he and a small group of subordinates, working without funds or an official charter, assembled a small fleet of helicopters, fitted them with borrowed machine guns and rockets, and carried out a series of freewheeling field tests. They practiced shooting under various conditions and honed newfound skills in nap-of-the-earth flying— the art of zipping along mere feet above the ground using trees and hills for concealment. Most onlookers were impressed, and word of the combat merits of helicopters began to spread in military circles.

But there was no lack of dissenters. The helicopter was widely viewed as too complex and vulnerable to rate a major combat role. Senator Mike Monroney of Oklahoma spoke for a sizable faction when he said, "I recognize it as an unusual and unique aircraft that puts you in places where you can't get into with fixed-wing or other aerial means. But I get kind of nervous when I read a UN helicopter over Africa was shot down by a bow and arrow." He saw little combat use for helicopters "other than hovering behind the line and doing a fine job of directing artillery fire or other jobs that could be done with a Piper Cub."

Part of the hesitancy to embrace helicopters stemmed from the Pentagon's assessment of the nature of future war. The most significant threat was thought to be an attack by masses of Soviet and Warsaw Pact armor on the plains of Europe. For such warfare, fixed-wing aircraft—with their advantages of higher speeds, greater payloads, and better resistance to groundfire—were thought to be much more suitable than the rotary-wing variety. Easily damaged helicopters, said military orthodoxy, were best suited for a lower-intensity conflict.

But rotary-wing aircraft had a few powerful advocates. One of them was General James Gavin, who had commanded the 82d Airborne Division during World World II, served in the Pentagon as Army chief of operations in the mid-1950s, and would round off his public career as U.S. ambassador to France. A polished and persuasive writer, Gavin would publish several influential articles on helicopter mobility, beginning in 1954. He suggested that the low-level air space over the presumed European combat zone—a region virtually closed to paratroops because of the potential adversaries' strength in antiaircraft weapons and tactical combat aircraft—was the very place for helicopters. They could operate well forward of friendly lines to identify and pinpoint targets for artillery and air strikes, and they could airlift troops quickly to key defensive points and provide logistical support. In one article, he looked back into military history and cited the potency of the cavalry of Alexander the Great, Roman legions marching along the strategic roads of the empire, and the German blitzkrieg in World War II—all of them strikingly innovative blends of force and mobility. He believed that helicopters held similar promise.

Events of June 24, 1956, at Tushino Airport in the Soviet Union, added fuel to his arguments. In a celebration of Soviet Air Force Day, the Russians stunned foreign observers with an awesome display of air power. A horde of low-flying helicopters burst into view and disgorged an assault force of troops, vehicles, and support weapons. While the troops carried out a mock attack, the helicopters roared away, then returned in waves carrying additional vehicles, ammunition, and fuel. The Soviets were practicing what General Gavin preached.

The Pentagon finally began to explore the possibilities of the helicopter in earnest when Secretary of Defense Robert McNamara punctured the prevailing conservatism with an impatient memorandum sent to the Secretary of the Army on April 19, 1962. He proposed the formation of a group to study tactical mobility, and he even listed several names that he expected to see on the membership roster, including—as chairman—Lieutenant General Hamilton Howze, then commander of XVIII Airborne Corps at Fort Bragg, North Carolina, which controlled all airborne forces based in the United States. The purpose, said McNamara, was to study "new organization and operational concepts, possibly including completely airmobile infantry, artillery, antitank, and reconnaissance units." The team, promptly constituted, was made up of fourteen generals and six civilians. Dubbed the Howze Board, it went to work at once and submitted a report four months later.

The document amounted to a call for a thorough overhaul of the Army. The Howze Board recommended that a third of the infantry divisions be airmobile. Each such division should replace about half of its 3,000 vehicles—trucks, tanks, self-propelled artillery, and so on—with about 330 helicopters. The report spelled out a vision of airmobile operations that included reconnaissance; calling in artillery fire; air assaults, in which troops arrive by helicopter to attack the enemy; and aerial supply lines. The Howze report emphasized that a battlefield must be seen three-dimensionally: "In the air just above the treetops lies one of the greatest hopes for victory on the ground." Now the ball was in the Army's court.

On a cold January morning in 1963, General Earl Wheeler, Army chief of staff, summoned to his office Brigadier General Harry Kinnard, assistant division commander of the 101st Airborne. "Harry,"

Wheeler said, "I want you to determine how far and how fast the Army can go and should go in embracing the airmobile concept." To accomplish this, Kinnard was to create an airmobile division at Fort Benning, Georgia—the 11th Air Assault Division (Test)—and use it to explore the issues and problems posed by the Howze Board recommendations.

Kinnard was an obvious choice for the job. A West Point graduate, he had parachuted into both Normandy and Holland during the Second World War as a battalion commander with the 101st Airborne. In his five months of combat, he earned the Distinguished Service Cross, the nation's second-highest medal for valor, and was promoted to full colonel at the age of twenty-nine—one of the youngest in the U.S. Army. Like James Gavin, Kinnard developed a strong interest in the helicopter the first time he encountered one. As he put it, he was "always searching at least subconsciously for a more sophisticated means of making a vertical descent than a parachute."

Kinnard began building his airmobility test unit from a base of about 3,000 soldiers (one-fifth the strength of a combat-ready division) and 125 helicopters. Some of the men had never even seen a helicopter. Training texts did not exist, and there were no standard operational techniques. The division had to work out methods of communication, modes of formation flying, and countless other basics—how to lash down cargo, how to disperse at a landing zone, how to rappel by rope from a helicopter to the ground

General Harry Kinnard, commander of the First Cavalry in Vietnam, watches his troops practice at the divisional base camp of An Khe in June 1966. Three years earlier, the resourceful former paratrooper had created a predecessor division at Fort Benning, Georgia, to develop many of the airmobility tactics and techniques that characterized the war in Vietnam.

Two CH-21 Shawnee helicopters flare for landing as they come in to pick up fresh ARVN paratroopers for a mission in the Mekong Delta only eight days after the destruction of five such choppers at Ap Bac. The eighty-foot-long, tandem-rotor Shawnee—dubbed the Flying Banana—cruised at a speed of 98 miles per hour and could carry about a dozen fully laden soldiers into combat. At right, the shattered carcass of a UH-1B Huey gunship lies on its side in a rice paddy after being shot down by heavy enemy ground-fire in January 1963. In the background rests a CH-21 Shawnee that shared a similar fate.

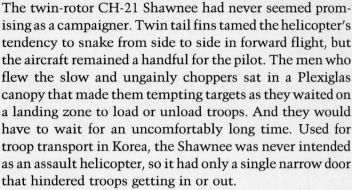

Not Quite Up to the Job

The twin-rotor CH-21 Shawnee had never seemed promising as a campaigner. Twin tail fins tamed the helicopter's tendency to snake from side to side in forward flight, but the aircraft remained a handful for the pilot. The men who flew the slow and ungainly choppers sat in a Plexiglas canopy that made them tempting targets as they waited on a landing zone to load or unload troops. And they would have to wait for an uncomfortably long time. Used for troop transport in Korea, the Shawnee was never intended as an assault helicopter, so it had only a single narrow door that hindered troops getting in or out.

The disaster that many observers feared would occur did so on January 3, 1963. As ten Shawnees flared for a landing at Ap Bac, a village in the Mekong Delta, the LZ erupted with heavy mortar, machine-gun, and automatic rifle fire. Five Huey gunships circling overhead tried valiantly to suppress the enemy fire with their skid-mounted 2.75-inch rockets and Gatling-style 7.62-mm Miniguns, but to no avail. Four of the CH-21s were destroyed. One of the gunships was hit, too, plunging to the ground in flames.

The Shawnee losses were a sobering experience for the small U.S. Army helicopter force in Vietnam, and although the incident temporarily shook American confidence in the concept of airmobility, that doubt would soon fade. But for the CH-21, the war was beginning to wind down. Within a few months of the fight at Ap Bac the first of the Shawnee's replacements—the faster, stronger UH-1B "slick"—would swing into action.

below, how to achieve surprise, how to deal with antiaircraft fire, how to refuel in the field, and so on. Kinnard himself was the source of an unending flow of ideas, and he had an insatiable hunger for more. He sought suggestions from all his troops, privates and colonels alike, and established an "ideas group" to evaluate an inundation of proposals.

Even as the test division was learning and perfecting its tactics, it began to receive a new generation of aircraft. The twin-rotor Boeing CH-47 Chinook supplied an unprecedented degree of heft: It could carry a 105-mm fieldpiece, plus ammunition, in a sling dangling below, or could haul forty-four men. The single-rotor Bell UH-1 Iroquois—which would become universally known as the Huey—was a sturdy, reliable, and agile general utility craft that could carry up to ten soldiers and a three-man crew. Kinnard's unit fitted the Huey with 3.5-inch rockets.

The standard assault drill devised by Kinnard's division aimed for maximum shock effect. Prior to the arrival of troops, artillery and

Carrying out the critical first step of an air assault during a demonstration in 1964 at Fort Benning, Georgia, Huey gunships clear the perimeter of a landing zone with fire simulated by small charges buried in the ground. The explosions, detonated manually from behind the spectators at the sound of the gunships shooting blanks, were so realistic that some of the observers scrambled from the grandstand in fear.

40

air strikes softened up the landing zone (the LZ, as it was called). As troopships headed into the LZ, the artillery stopped firing, and the rocket-firing gunships took over. Chinooks could shift the artillery to more advantageous positions, if necessary, and other helicopters stood by to resupply the troops, evacuate the wounded and bring in replacements, and extract the force when it had finished its work. The airmobile commander directed all this activity from a control helicopter flying 3,000 feet above the fray.

Kinnard conducted a long series of field tests, climaxing in one of the largest post-World War II maneuvers ever staged in the United States. This thirty-day trial, held during October and November of 1964 in a leased area of 4.5 million acres stretching from Fayetteville, North Carolina, to Columbia, South Carolina, pitted the airmobile test division against the famed 82d Airborne, reinforced. The contest involved some initial sparring, followed by defensive and offensive phases, a night attack, and other tests in a variety of situations. Some of

the maneuvers were conducted as a severe storm moved through the Carolinas. On deep penetration raids, the helicopters roared in just above the treetops, hit the opposition, and then withdrew, only to strike again and again. On the defense against heavily armed ground troops, the airmobile forces melted back while counter-punching with gunships.

The referees were impressed. Regardless of the tactical situation, the airmobile division proved that its elements could seek out an enemy over a large area and then rapidly bring together the necessary firepower and troops to defeat the enemy. While the division's ground mobility was not particularly good and its vulnerability to armor was something of a problem, Kinnard's troops could simultaneously fight in several directions, could react quickly, and could carry out their operations at an extraordinarily high tempo. The Army recommended that the test division move to the active list. On June 28, 1965, McNamara effectively took that step. The 11th Air Assault Division (Test) was deactivated, and, by exchanges of divisional colors, its men and equipment were transferred to the First Division, now to be known as the First Cavalry Division.

The secretary of defense had another piece of news: Kinnard was to prepare his 16,000-man force to go to Vietnam. Just weeks earlier, a gloomy report on the war there had come from General William Westmoreland, the commander on the scene. The enemy's spring offensive, said Westmoreland, had been devastating. Westmoreland judged that South Vietnam could not "stand up successfully to this kind of pressure." In response, President Lyndon Johnson authorized the deployment of 200,000 combat troops to Southeast Asia. The First Cav, whose 400 helicopters exceeded the number of aircraft that South Vietnam possessed at the time, would be the first full-strength Army division to go.

In late October 1965, barely three weeks after the First Cavalry Division had hacked out a base for itself at An Khe in the central highlands of South Vietnam, there occurred in the plateau country southwest of Pleiku City a series of skirmishes and larger actions that would become known as the Pleiku campaign or (after the valley in which many were fought) the Ia Drang battles. Airmobile tactics that had been developed piecemeal at Fort Benning would now be tested in a real war.

Early in the year, the 32d Regiment of the North Vietnamese Army (NVA) had filtered out of Cambodia along the Ho Chi Minh network of trails into South Vietnam. The 33d NVA Regiment followed in September, and the 66th Regiment was on its way. Together, the three regiments constituted an entire division, the largest massing of North Vietnamese strength since the fall of the French military base of Dien Bien Phu to insurgents in 1954—an event that ended France's hold on its Indochina colony.

The assembled forces were commanded by Brigadier General Chu Huy Man, who intended to inflict on the Republic of Vietnam and its American backers a defeat as crushing and final as Dien Bien Phu had been. He positioned his force along the eastern slopes of the Chu Pong Massif, a formation of mountains that rose above the Ia Drang Valley, about halfway between the South China Sea and Cambodia. The highlands were wild and desolate, a ravine-slashed region of scrub and huge termite hills, virtually empty except for tigers, elephants, and scattered Montagnard tribesmen. Here, taking advantage of the rugged area's remoteness and the difficulty of defending it, Chu planned to slice South Vietnam in half.

To do so, Chu had to capture Pleiku, a provincial capital, and then drive eastward to the port city of Qui Nhon. The first step of his campaign would be to knock out two U.S. Army Special Forces camps that lay in his path. These installations—located near the villages of Plei Me, thirty miles due south of Pleiku, and Duc Co, eight miles from Cambodia on Highway 19, a well-traveled dirt or gravel road that ran east and west through Pleiku City to Qui Nhon—were actually small fish, but their destruction would have considerable propaganda value. Moreover, attacking them might lure South Vietnamese troops into an ambush.

An hour before midnight on the nineteenth of October, 82-mm mortar shells fired by the 33d NVA Regiment began exploding inside the Plei Me camp, followed by machine-gun and small-arms fire. The battle was on. Reluctantly—and certain of being waylaid—an ARVN reaction force set out from Pleiku by road in a column of tanks, armored personnel carriers, and towed 105-mm howitzers.

In the meantime, General Kinnard sent a battalion-size task force of the First Cav to reinforce the defenses at Pleiku, knowing that the city was Chu's real objective. He had also gained permission from General Westmoreland in Saigon to go to the aid of the South Vietnamese relief column—but only if it requested help, since the United States was operating on the premise that the war was still a Vietnamese show.

The ARVN column, proceeding with great caution on its thirty-mile march to Plei Me, was still six miles from its goal on October 23 when the 32d NVA Regiment struck. To the surprise of the North Vietnamese, who had little respect for the fighting capabilities of their enemy, the South Vietnamese troops resisted fiercely and drove back the assault. However, the ARVN commander, even though he could hear the sounds of battle at Plei Me in the distance, refused to go farther until he was provided artillery support.

Kinnard seized this opportunity. On October 24, sky troopers of the First Cavalry's First Brigade began the first real airmobile operation of the campaign when they dropped onto landing zones ahead of the ARVN's route of march and then flew in artillery pieces slung beneath the bellies of Chinook helicopters.

With two batteries of First Cav howitzers dropping shells along the road in front of them, the ARVN troops continued their advance. General Chu, taken aback by the helicopters' injection of heavy firepower into the fray, realized he had lost his opportunity to overrun Plei Me. He withdrew toward a longtime Vietcong stronghold in the Ia Drang Valley. This area was so remote and so infested with enemy troops that the South Vietnamese Army had never dared to enter it. To cover his retreat, he left a delaying force around the Plei Me camp. Chu had suffered his first defeat.

When First Cav troopers reached Plei Me on October 27, they were shocked. The camp had been pounded and ripped apart by shell and rocket fire. The smell of putrefying flesh hung like a pall over the countryside. Soon, the First Cavalry suffered its first casualty of the campaign: Staff Sergeant Charles Rose died from a sniper's bullet while leading his squad up a hill south of the camp to clear it of any remaining enemy.

On the afternoon of October 26, the scope of First Cavalry operations changed from reinforcement and reaction to unlimited offense. Addressing a high-level conference of ranking officers chaired by General Westmoreland in Saigon, Kinnard insisted that the enemy must be sought aggressively. Now was the time to begin, before the NVA force that had threatened Plei Me could refit and regroup. After Kinnard made his pitch, Westmoreland turned to General Stanley Larsen, who oversaw the First Cav as commander of I Field Force, an entity comprising several American units. "Give Kinnard his head," Westmoreland said. "I think the Cav is ready." The mission was defined in starkly simple terms: "Find, fix, and destroy the enemy forces threatening Plei Me, Pleiku, and the central highlands."

One by one over the next month, Kinnard would put all three brigades of his division into the fight and let them use their newly forged skills to the full. This was a war that demanded mobility of the most supple and quick-reflexed kind—a war without clearly delineated front lines and a rear support area, a war of attrition rather than territorial gains, a hide-and-seek war fought on terrain that could almost have been designed to frustrate ground vehicles.

Kinnard's assault units used a three-team organization for search-and-destroy. In each company-size outfit, a so-called White Team, flying ten bubble-nosed OH-13 Sioux helicopters, was charged with finding the enemy. A successful search brought a Red Team into action: It consisted of ten Huey gunships, armed with rockets and machine guns, that cleared the area around a landing zone and subsequently provided supporting fire. To tackle a small enemy force, set up an ambush, or secure the LZ for the arrival of additional sky soldiers, a Blue Team of Huey troop carriers—called slicks because, unlike gunships, they had no externally mounted guns or rockets that increased aerodynamic drag—inserted a rifle platoon of about twenty infantrymen.

During the last week of October, the reconnaissance helicopters probed every corner of the tumbled and tangled region, nosing right down to treetop level for a look at trails or other signs of activity, constantly harassing Chu's withdrawing forces. The choppers re-

Troops of the First Cav survey the devastation wrought by North Vietnamese artillery during an attack on a Special Forces camp at Plei Me in October 1965. Thwarted by the quick reaction of airmobile reinforcements, the North Vietnamese retreated toward a sanctuary along the Cambodian border, still intent on a plan to deliver a decisive blow in the war by cutting South Vietnam in half.

For most of the war in Vietnam, U.S. helicopters flew in skies relatively free from enemy fire. But with time, VC and NVA forces began to mount a greater threat to airmobile operations. Helicopters were most vulnerable when they descended to deliver or retrieve troops. For chopper crews, extracting soldiers from "hot" LZs alive with enemy fire became the most hazardous task of all.

While circling gunships provided fire support from above, troop-carrying slicks often had to descend into determined enemy fire to pluck the stranded soldiers from their predicament *(left)*. Often these missions succeeded, with largely inconsequential

A UH-1 Huey, its door gunner firing at a well-concealed enemy, prepares to extract troops of the 173d Airborne Brigade pinned down near the Ai Lao River in Binh Dinh Province on March 29, 1970. Such rescue missions were frequent, necessary, and fraught with danger.

damage to the helicopters. At other times, the toll on the choppers was a heavy one.

In March 1971, when U.S. helicopters were sent to evacuate troops from a stalled ARVN advance into Laos known as Operation Lam Son 719, the NVA employed more firepower than had yet been seen in the war. Slick pilots braved rocket, mortar, and machine-gun fire to hover six or seven feet off the ground while aircrews pulled the panicked soldiers aboard. "If you got on the ground," a crewman recalled, "they would turn the helicopter over." In desperation, some ARVN troops grabbed the skids and made it back to South Vietnam dangling below the already overloaded choppers.

Hundreds of flights over a fifty-three-day period were needed to extract the troops and return them to South Vietnam. The cost: 107 helicopters shot down, more than in any other airmobile operation of the war.

peatedly drew enemy fire, but the North Vietnamese found both the OH-13s and the bigger Hueys difficult to bring down. Few were hit, partly because of NVA inexperience in dealing with them and partly because of the First Cav's fast-moving, low-flying tactics.

On October 29, a Blue Team force landed right in the middle of an enemy cache of weapons and food, killing sixteen NVA soldiers, capturing eight, and wounding twelve. Three days later, on November 1, a rifle platoon commanded by Captain John Oliver surprised a regimental aid station along the Tae River, about seven miles west of Plei Me. The platoon killed fifteen NVA soldiers and captured the hospital and a large store of medicines.

When the enemy counterattacked with a battalion, Oliver formed a tight defensive perimeter around a small clearing uphill from the aid station. Over the next two and a half hours, two companies of reinforcements—about 200 men—were fed into the fight, sometimes arriving one bird at a time in Oliver's tiny clearing above the streambed while gunships hammered at surrounding NVA soldiers to keep them pinned down. Eight helicopters were hit, but all of them continued flying. One of the pilots, Chief Warrant Officer David Ankerberg, would receive the Distinguished Flying Cross for delivering much-needed ammunition, braving intense groundfire that scored eleven hits on his chopper.

This was the first major action of the Pleiku campaign. The sky soldiers stopped the NVA counterattack cold and quickly regained the offensive. When the elements of the NVA 33d withdrew in defeat the next morning, they left ninety-nine dead soldiers on the field; many more fatalities were presumably carried away, as was the enemy's custom. The First Cav casualties were eleven dead and fifty-one wounded.

Despite this setback, General Chu was determined to have his victory. The fresh 66th NVA Regiment slipped into the fight against Kinnard's sky soldiers, giving the North Vietnamese a substantial edge in numbers. But the helicopter was proving to be what military planners called a force multiplier—a technological advantage that changed the odds. Over and over again, the NVA discovered that their old notions of the enemy's firepower and mobility no longer applied.

On the afternoon of November 3, four platoons of the First Cav established a patrol base on a hilltop clearing north of the Chu Pong Massif and sent three platoon-size ambush forces into the enemy stronghold of the Ia Drang Valley. One of these platoons, commanded by Captain Charles Knowlen, was lying in wait after dark along a trail when the men heard the sound of troops on the move. The NVA felt so secure in the area that they were talking and laughing. A heavy-weapons company, lead element of the newly arrived 66th Regiment, stopped close by to take a break, its point man just fifteen feet from where Sergeant Eugene Pennington hid in the moonlit underbrush. "I'll never understand how they missed seeing me," he later said.

After about twenty-five minutes, the enemy column began moving again in the bright moonlight. Pennington counted forty-eight soldiers carrying small arms, followed by a group carrying mortars, recoilless rifles, and machine guns. Knowlen let them get close, then triggered ten claymore mines that together sent thousands of steel pellets slashing through the NVA troops. The ambush was so devastating that the enemy did not fire a single shot in return. Knowlen's platoon beat a hasty retreat, covered by mortar fire from their patrol base. No sooner had the platoon reached the base than the North Vietnamese attacked in battalion strength.

Now the night-flying skills practiced back in the United States came into play. A company of reinforcements landed in the clearing in six-helicopter lots. The first lift, escorted by a Red Team of armed helicopters, swept in under the light of flares. Subsequent runs used only the light of the full moon. A platoon leader dubbed the landing zone LZ Spiderweb because the sky was crisscrossed by a brilliant pyrotechnical webbing of red tracers fired by the Americans and bluish green tracers from the NVA weapons.

Once again, because of the quick American reactions, General Chu lost what should have been an easy victory against outnumbered U.S. forces. Instead, the battalion that was sent to eliminate the patrol base suffered seventy-two dead by actual body count. Two Americans had died.

For the remainder of the first two weeks of November, Kinnard's sky soldiers continued their relentless pursuit of the North Vietnamese. By November 7, when Kinnard began to withdraw the First Brigade and replace it with Colonel Thomas Brown's Third Brigade, the 33d NVA Regiment alone had lost, by U.S. intelligence estimates, about 900 of its original 2,200 men. American losses so far were 59 dead, 196 wounded.

The decisive battle of the campaign, the ultimate test of airmobility against ground infantry, was about to occur around an opening in the trees, no more than 100 meters long, that nestled near the foot of one of the mountains of the Chu Pong Massif. When White Team helicopters, dipping below treetop level, spotted well-used trails and communications wire nearby, no one suspected the size of the force in the vicinity. As it happened, the clearing that would gain fame as LZ X-Ray was located almost on top of the headquarters and staging area for Chu's regiments.

The climactic events began shortly after dawn on November 14 when the First Battalion of the First Cav's Seventh Regiment, commanded by Lieutenant Colonel Harold Moore, was ordered to X-Ray as the starting point for a search-and-destroy mission. Moore's plan was straightforward. Artillery and gunships would clear any opposition from the landing zone first (to confuse the enemy, artillery would also fire at two neighboring clearings called Tango and Yankee). The battalion's four companies would then be landed at X-Ray; one company would secure the LZ while the others fanned out to scour the area.

Moore was first out the door of the first chopper to touch down. Right behind him came elements of the 119-man B Company, who sprinted toward the line of trees firing their rifles to see if they could get any response from any enemy troops who might be hiding there. The Huey transports lifted out of the clearing, and a

Helicopter Assault at LZ X-Ray

Descending across a landscape cratered by artillery fire, the First Battalion of the U.S. Seventh Cavalry Regiment sets down in a small landing zone at the base of the Chu Pong Massif, a mountain bastion held by the North Vietnamese in regimental strength.

As the last of three four-ship groups of UH-1D Huey transports, or slicks, approaches the small clearing, two UH-1B Huey gunships blast the LZ perimeter with 7.62-mm machine-gun fire and 2.75-inch rockets. The slicks are flying in a "heavy left" formation. By placing three of the four Hueys near the trees edging the left of the LZ, the arrangement let transport door gunners spray suspected enemy positions in the trees. Ahead of the approaching slicks, an earlier flight of four transports is ready to depart, having required less than fifteen seconds to land and disembark the passengers. Meanwhile, the first four slicks to arrive, having dropped off battalion commander Lieutenant Colonel Harold Moore and twenty additional troopers, have taken off and are banking steeply toward the Special Forces camp at Plei Me to pick up reinforcements.

Another Huey *(not shown)*, circling 2,000 feet above the landing zone, serves as an airborne fire-control center. Inside the chopper, the battalion operations officer, an assault-helicopter liaison officer, a forward air controller, and a fire support coordinator direct artillery and air strikes against the hundreds of enemy troops that threaten to engulf the battalion.

second wave of helicopters arrived. But because only eight helicopters at a time could land, four hours would pass before the entire battalion could be inserted.

Meanwhile, four six-man squads set forth in different directions, ordered to reconnoiter a distance of about a hundred yards into the trees. Within minutes, one of the squads captured an NVA deserter. He said that he had been living off bananas for the past five days. Then he pointed up the Chu Pong slope. "There are three battalions on the mountain who want very much to kill Americans but haven't been able to find any," he said.

At 12:30 p.m., as A Company landed on X-Ray and assumed responsibility from the earlier arrivals for securing it, the platoons of B Company spread out to explore the ground toward the Chu Pong heights. The twenty-seven-man Second Platoon was led by Lieutenant Henry Herrick, an impetuous soldier fresh out of officer's training when he was assigned to the First Cav about a month before the division departed for Vietnam.

Herrick's platoon spotted a handful of enemy troops and charged off in pursuit. They ran head-on into about 150 North Vietnamese pouring down the slope. The rest of B Company was about 125 yards to the left—too far away to help. Herrick's platoon was soon surrounded and pinned down. The lieutenant pulled his men into a circle about twenty-five yards across and prepared to hold out. He was killed immediately.

Command passed to the platoon sergeant, Carl Palmer, who had commented to another soldier that morning, "I'll be forty-three years old tomorrow, but I don't believe I'll live to see it." He died minutes later, first wounded with a bullet through the skull and killed shortly thereafter by a grenade. Buck Sergeant Ernie Savage took over. Eight soldiers had been killed and twelve wounded within the first minutes of the fight, leaving only seven unscathed. Savage grabbed a radio and began calling artillery fire around his position.

While survivors of that platoon fought for their lives, platoons of A Company on X-Ray battled waves of khaki-clad NVA regulars in pith helmets. Through the rest of the day and night, troops from Chu's 33d and 66th regiments attempted to break the Americans' perimeter. Meanwhile, at the Brigade Operations Center, Kinnard and Colonel Brown orchestrated their airmobile resources. As part of the plan for the operation, Chinooks had airlifted two batteries of 105-mm howitzers—twelve guns in all—to LZ Falcon, a clearing about five miles east of the battle. During the two nights the battle would span, artillery at LZ Falcon would pump more than 4,400 rounds of high explosives into the fight. Many fell within fifty meters of the X-Ray perimeter in an effort to prevent NVA troops from getting "into a bear hug with us," Moore later said, to prevent the use of artillery and other fire support. Between artillery barrages came flights of Navy, Marine, and Air Force fighter-bombers to bomb, strafe, and napalm enemy positions. Huey transports, escorted by gunships pouring 7.62-mm machine-gun fire and 2.75-inch rockets into the trees, continued to bring in reinforcements and supplies and to carry out the wounded. Major Bruce Crandall flew two choppers on the fourteenth, his first being damaged when he clipped some trees while hauling out wounded. On one flight, the North Vietnamese blazed away at his helicopter from almost point-blank range; his crew chief was shot in the throat.

X-Ray was a scene of mayhem. Choppers rose and descended through dust and smoke; exploding artillery shells and rockets hammered at the air; and staccato bursts of machine-gun and rifle fire mixed with the screams and shouts of the combatants. Machine gunner Bill Beck almost single-handedly blocked the enemy on one line of approach: "They were shooting at me, bullets hitting the ground beside me and cracking above my head. I was firing as fast as I could in long bursts."

An NVA machine gun positioned on a termite mound threatened to wipe out a Company B platoon just beyond the edge of the clearing. Lieutenant Joe Marm, after trying to destroy the weapon with an antitank rocket, charged across twenty-five yards of open ground, threw a grenade behind the hill, then moved around its side and let loose with his rifle. A sniper's bullet smashed into his jaw, exiting through his throat, but medics would be able to save him. He had destroyed the machine gun and killed a dozen of the enemy—a feat that would earn him the Medal of Honor. Asked later why he had charged the machine gun, Marm said: "To get the job done and save time."

By nightfall, the Americans were well dug in all around the clearing, and mortars and artillery had been calibrated to drop shells within twenty-five yards of their lines. Helicopters stopped shuttling in and out of the LZ at ten o'clock. Some of the pilots had been flying for sixteen hours straight. "When I tried to get out of the aircraft,'' said Bruce Crandall, "it caught up with me. My legs gave out, and I fell to the ground vomiting and shaking." The inside of his helicopter was awash with the blood of the wounded.

The Second Platoon of Company B was still cut off. Three NVA attacks would be hurled against it during the night, one of them presaged by bugle calls from the Chu Pong heights, but Sergeant Ernie Savage's little band held on.

Having slackened their efforts during the night, the NVA struck hard at first light on November 15, sending a force estimated at 1,000 against the X-Ray perimeter. One American who manned a machine gun later said, "I looked to the front, and it seemed like the North Vietnamese were growing out of the weeds. The training took over. I just fired that weapon, totally unaware of the time, the conditions. I remember a lot of noise, a lot of yelling, air strikes." Fighting was so furious—including vicious hand-to-hand combat in some places—that midmorning arrived before the battle waned sufficiently for helicopters to begin landing a company of reinforcements from An Khe. A larger, battalion-size unit landed at a clearing two miles away and started a forced march to flank the enemy and relieve X-Ray. By noon, they reached the battlefield. One soldier said, "My God, there's enemy bodies all over this valley. For the last thirty minutes, we've been walking around and over and through bodies."

The North Vietnamese continued to attack until ten in the morn-

On the third day of the battle at Landing Zone X-Ray, First Cavalry riflemen fire their M16s as they advance cautiously through elephant grass at the base of the Chu Pong Massif. That day, the enemy force on the mountain, already hard hit from the air by ground-attack fighters and helicopter gunships, would be subjected to history's first close-support hammering by B-52 strategic bombers.

ing, when they withdrew under fire. As they pulled back, they dragged away their wounded and some of their dead. Yet scores of corpses and weapons were left to litter the battleground.

Shortly after three that afternoon, a rescue force from X-Ray fought its way to the position of the trapped Second Platoon. Amazingly, no casualties had been suffered since Sergeant Savage took over. By half past four, the survivors and the dead were back on X-Ray. That night, the NVA returned to the fight and continued it into the next day. At intervals, the North Vietnamese commanders threw hundreds of soldiers against the First Cavalry's position, but the opportunity had passed. By that time, Moore had been reinforced in battalion strength and amply resupplied with ammunition. In the end, the American firepower—climaxed by the bombing of the Chu Pong heights by B-52s based on Guam—proved too much for the North Vietnamese. General Chu's command was all but destroyed. The body count of NVA dead was 634; additional dead and wounded were estimated at more than 1,200. American casualties were listed as 79 killed, 121 wounded.

After the battle at X-Ray, Kinnard requested permission to pursue the enemy into Cambodia. His request was approved by General Westmoreland and by U.S. Ambassador Henry Cabot Lodge, but it was denied in Washington. Still, Kinnard had ample reason for

A First Cav trooper sprints from his Huey to retrieve the body of a fallen comrade, spotted while the helicopter was flying over LZ X-Ray. By then, the Americans had withdrawn, but their commander had vowed to leave no dead behind.

satisfaction. His First Cav had more than lived up to the expectations of airmobility advocates such as Gavin and Howze. From October 23 to November 28, 1965, the First Cavalry Division had played a pivotal role in rescuing the Plei Me Special Forces camp. In hot pursuit of General Chu's forces, Kinnard's sky soldiers had applied new airmobile tactics to chase the enemy back to its stronghold in the Ia Drang Valley and then, outnumbered seven to one, to win a huge victory. In doing so, the First Cav moved complete infantry companies 193 times, conducted 6,000 sorties, logged 27,000 hours of flying time, airlifted 13,000 tons of supplies, moved entire artillery batteries 67 times, provided close air support, conducted reconnaissance missions—and virtually obliterated two of North Vietnam's best infantry regiments. Only four cavalry helicopters were shot down during that period, and three of them were recovered to fly again.

From the baptism by fire at X-Ray until America completed its withdrawal from Vietnam on April 29, 1975, airmobility would be the defining characteristic of the war. To planners in Washington, airmobile infantry conducting search-and-destroy missions seemed the long-sought key to winning in Vietnam. Westmoreland expressed his belief that U.S. troops such as the First Cav "will give us a substantial and hard-hitting offensive capability on the ground to convince the VC that they cannot win." And so, Vietnam became the Helicopter War. By the late 1960s, more than 2,000 Hueys would be in the air over Vietnam on any given day.

Inevitably, however, the Vietcong and North Vietnamese adjusted to the new challenge, much as did the Algerians fighting against the French. They learned how to fire at choppers flying overhead, how to mine likely landing zones, how to lure sky soldiers into ambushes. During the course of the war, a total of 4,112 helicopters were downed, and five of the eight generals who were killed in Vietnam died in helicopters. Nonetheless, Vietnam changed modern warfare. By the late 1960s, every branch of the U.S. armed forces—and the forces of other nations as well—had taken to the sky in rotary-wing aircraft. Back in 1962, the Howze Board had declared that the helicopter could bring about a tactical revolution "as profound as the mechanization of warfare by the gasoline engine." That bold prophecy had proved correct. ★

3

Great Expectations in Afghanistan

Working hand in glove with airborne troops, the VDV, in Afghanistan, the Mi-24 Hind attack helicopter became a symbol of a war that the Soviets ultimately abandoned. Though menacing with its arsenal of four 57-mm rocket pods and a three-barreled 12.7-mm machine gun under the nose, the Hind was not invincible. An estimated 300 of them were lost in the war, about half to heavy machine guns and portable surface-to-air missiles.

In August 1985, the Soviet Union's best-trained, best-equipped airborne forces put on a textbook display of their potency. The scene was a desolate locale in eastern Afghanistan, close to the border with Pakistan. Because of the border's hooked shape there, the place is known as the Parrot's Beak. Towering mountains, some more than 15,000 feet high, barricade the area, and paved roads are nonexistent. Here lurked thousands of Mujahedin—guerrillas who had been fighting since 1979 to reclaim their nation from Soviet occupiers and a puppet government. For their opportunistic, hit-and-run style of warfare, the Parrot's Beak was an ideal base of operations. In addition to the region's inaccessibility to enemy armor, it was close to sanctuary in Pakistan, where the guerrillas could rest and resupply—and it lay just thirty miles from the their ultimate target, the Afghan capital of Kabul. But danger was approaching. The guerrilla bastion was about to be breached by the the Red Army's elite sky soldiers—the Vozdushno-Desantnyye Voiska, or Air Assault Force. Intended for large-scale war in Europe or against China, the VDV, like American airmobile forces beginning in the mid-1960s, now applied its skills to an entirely different kind of battle.

Altogether, 20,000 troops—half Soviet, half Afghan—were sent against the Mujahedin. Beginning on August 20, three task forces composed of conventional infantry advanced overland toward the guerrilla stronghold from different directions. Then, as these columns approached the Parrot's Beak, the VDV arrived by air. Dozens of helicopters carrying a regiment of paratroops from bases around Kabul swept down on nine landing zones and threw a cordon around villages and Mujahedin bases at the head of one of the valleys stretching away from the mountain fastness. When the landing zones were secured, the paratroops went hunting for the guerrillas with assault rifles, grenade launchers, machine guns, and antitank rockets, which were good for flushing the guerrillas from defensive bunkers. Mi-24 Hind attack helicopters swept out of the sky, hammering at the encircled quarry with cannon fire and rockets. At least a hundred Mujahedin died as the noose was tightened. Meanwhile, other heliborne troops surrounded Mujahedin camps farther north, seizing weapons caches and critical stores of grain. By the conclusion of the operation in mid-September, the attacking forces had fought their way to the heart of the Parrot's Beak and compelled large numbers of Mujahedin to retreat into Pakistan. Some of the guerrilla bases in the area withstood the assault, but the helicopter invasion of the mountain refuge had dealt the Afghan freedom fighters a heavy blow, one they would long remember.

Unfortunately for the Kremlin, there were too few such punches. In the course of a nine-year war, Soviet troops—about 120,000 at any moment, and a large percentage of them airborne—fought alongside a similar number of Afghan government soldiers against a motley army of indifferent skill that had poorer weapons and lacked a central command. Yet the Mujahedin had significant assets—religious and patriotic fervor, the support of most of the population, and an intimate knowledge of terrain that posed immense problems for conventional military forces. In the end, the Soviets would withdraw from the fight, bloodied and dispirited. Afghanistan, many observers said, was their Vietnam, a bitter lesson in the difficulties of counterinsurgency warfare. But for the VDV, the war was in many ways a validation, repeatedly demonstrating the tactical advantages of airmobile warfare and confirming the reputation of the airborne force as one of the toughest, most resourceful instruments of Soviet military power.

That reputation is rooted deep in the annals of twentieth-century warfare. The VDV was the world's first air-assault force, conceived in the late 1920s by a leading Soviet military theoretician, General Mikhail Tukhachevsky. In exercises held in August 1930, he supplied dramatic proof of the merits of a three-dimensional approach to the battlefield by dropping a detachment of twelve paratroops onto a divisional headquarters, taking it utterly by surprise and causing general chaos. Onlookers were greatly impressed.

By 1934, he had built the Soviet airborne force to some 10,000 men. Such rapid growth was possible, in part, because the state encouraged parachuting as a sport, erecting jumping towers near large cities. Leaping from a plane—generally the Red Air Force's first four-engine bomber, the Tupolev TB-3—was an altogether more challenging matter, of course. The exit technique consisted of crawling from inside the fuselage onto the bomber's wing by means of handles, then sliding off into free fall. In 1935, two paratroop regiments displayed their wing-walking method in an exercise held near Kiev. Said a British observer: "It was a most spectacular performance." Another member of the audience, General Kurt Student of Germany, was no less dazzled; he would soon form an airborne division for the Luftwaffe.

Tukhachevsky's abilities as an innovator and organizer could not save him from Stalin's army purges in the late 1930s; he, like most of the Soviet High Command, was executed. But his military creation survived. By mid-1941, when Germany invaded the Soviet Union, the airborne contingent had grown to five full corps, each with 10,000 men. Viewed as the elite among the forces defending Mother Russia, the units were all given the title Guards—an honorific retained by the eight divisions constituting the VDV today.

During the years of desperate fighting to save the homeland, paratroops mostly served in both airborne and conventional infantry roles. Besides conducting hundreds of small diversionary attacks and reconnaissance missions, airborne troops occasionally mounted huge operations. In early 1942, for example, the better part of two airborne corps—16,000 men—conducted extensive operations in the German rear area. One corps tied down five German divisions for more than four months. The paratroops suffered heavy casualties, but the majority survived to rejoin Soviet main forces.

Not every undertaking was so successful. One especially costly venture took place at Kanev in September 1943. With the Germans in retreat all along the eastern front, the Soviet High Command sought to trap the 24th Panzer Corps by a massive two-night airdrop. Beyond snaring a sizable portion of the Wehrmacht's vaunted armored forces, the goal of the operation was to secure a bridgehead across the Dnieper River so that Soviet ground forces could press their offensive and drive the enemy out of the Ukraine. The Soviets marshaled some 235 transport aircraft to parachute men and matériel and a glider fleet to deliver artillery.

Although the essence of the Soviet plan was to beat the Germans to the other side of the river, the entire panzer force managed to rumble across unmolested. Not until dusk—when the Germans

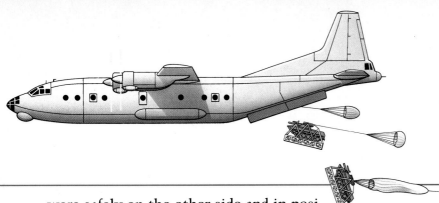

were safely on the other side and in position to intercept the Soviet airborne force—did the first Soviet planes appear. The transports, carrying a brigade of paratroops, flew in perfect formation. At an altitude of 2,000 feet, with their landing lights on, they proved to be easy targets for antiaircraft guns. Those that were not hit dropped their charges into a murderous cross fire or carried them far off target; one unfortunate group landed right in the path of an approaching panzer column. When the magnitude of the disaster became apparent, the Soviets canceled the second wave of troop transports as well as the artillery-laden gliders—leaving what remained of the first 7,000-man contingent to fend for itself against the more heavily armed German force. More than half of the VDV trapped on the unfriendly side of the Dnieper perished.

During the war, the VDV participated in one more operation, intended to hasten Japan's surrender. In 1945, shortly before V-J Day, a score of airborne groups, some as large as 500 men, were landed at key Japanese airfields in Manchuria as other Soviet troops mounted a strong ground offensive. In all twenty actions, the paratroops persuaded numerically superior Japanese garrisons to surrender—an unparalleled cluster of successes.

The war's lessons about air-assault operations were plain: Paratroops could be highly effective if able to make an uncontested landing on a suitable drop zone in fair weather. But large-scale airborne attacks against heavy opposition would likely result in disaster, especially in bad weather, unless coordinated with a large and successful offensive on the ground.

During the late 1940s and 1950s, as the Soviet Union increasingly devoted its attention and resources to acquiring a nuclear arsenal, the VDV languished. In 1956, the airborne force was changed from an autonomous organization in the Soviet military scheme to a special branch of the Soviet Army. To set them off from the regular infantry, the VDV acquired distinctive new attire—a dashing blue beret and a blue-and-white-striped T-shirt.

In the late 1960s—and coinciding with the emergence of the helicopter as an alternative to the parachute for airmobility—military planners in the USSR decided to revitalize the Soviet Union's ability to fight a conventional, nonnuclear war. In 1966, an influential article appeared in the Soviet journal *Military Thought*. Written by

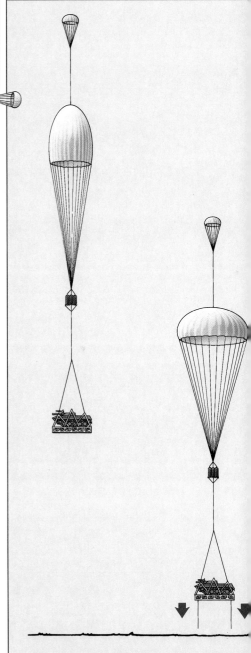

The Soviets have developed an ingenious method of airdropping the BMD infantry fighting vehicle. A drogue parachute pulls the vehicle—secured on a pallet—clear of the aircraft. The jolt of the main chute popping open extends four sensor rods fixed to the bottom of the pallet. Contact with the ground fires a rocket attached to the chute, which slows the vehicle's descent and greatly softens the landing. This technique greatly reduces the number of BMDs damaged as a result of airdrops.

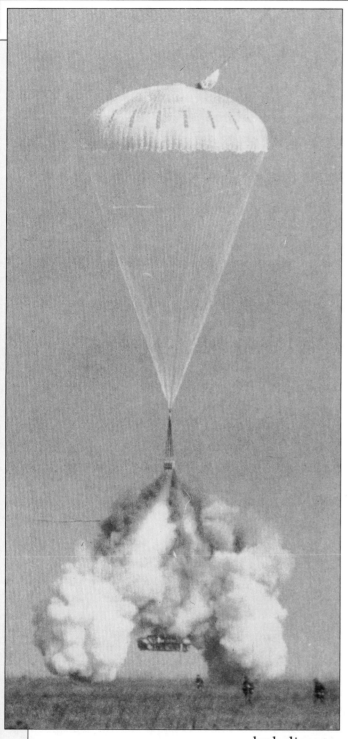

two General Staff colonels, the treatise took a close look at the basic operational concept of the VDV and concluded that modification was in order.

Historically, the role of Soviet paratroopers, like those of other nations, was to drop in the enemy's rear or on the flank, seize critical objectives—airfields, bridges, weapons depots, communications centers, and so on—and hold on until ground forces could join them. An airborne assault of this kind was known as a desant, from a Russian word meaning "descent." Since the paratroops would be on foot and lightly armed, relieving forces had to come to their aid quickly, before enemy armor could overwhelm them. Nuclear war, where concentrations of tanks could be destroyed quickly with one or two weapons before they could threaten isolated airborne units, would somewhat reduce the urgency of relief and extend the distance behind enemy lines that paratroops could fight. But in conventional battle, the need for timely assistance clearly restricted the depth to which an air assault could strike.

The authors of the 1966 article recommended much greater independence for the VDV. "An airborne force transported to the deep rear of the enemy must be able to conduct military operations without counting on linking up with ground troops. The troops that make up the force will need the same qualities that are inherent in troops attacking from the front: a high degree of maneuverability and the possession of all types of weapons, equipment, and matériel necessary to conduct long-range military operations." Whether inserted by parachute, by helicopter, or by landing at an airfield, they needed the firepower and mobility to hold their gains without assistance.

The upshot of this bold redefinition—put into effect over the next two decades—was the world's first fully mechanized airborne force. Today, the VDV has a total strength estimated at 100,000 men organized into eight Guards airborne divisions and seven or more independent air-assault brigades.

Each of the divisions is assigned 330 BMD armored fighting vehicles. The workhorse BMD mounts three 7.62-mm machine guns, antitank guided missiles, and either a 30-mm or a 73-mm automatic cannon. Lightly armored, it is designed to carry a six-man squad plus a three-man crew. In addition to its BMDs, each division also has fifty four-wheel amphibious reconnaissance vehicles, armed with machine guns and antitank guided missiles—plus self-propelled 120-mm mortars that can be used against area targets or armored vehicles. Any of this equipment can be slung under a helicopter or parachuted from a plane. For an airdrop, a vehicle is set on a special pallet equipped with retrorockets that cushion the landing *(pages 62-63)*. At the same time, a radio beacon mounted on the dropped vehicle is activated to signal its location.

While the Guards divisions deploy in conventional air transports, the air-assault brigades rely for mobility exclusively on rotary-wing aircraft. Unlike American airmobile forces, however, Soviet airborne units have no helicopters of their own. Instead, they call on the chopper fleet of the Soviet Air Force to provide transportation and firepower. The mainstays of VDV helicopter operations range from the Mi-17 Hip, which can carry ninety troops into battle, to the deadly Mi-24 Hind gunship, armed with machine guns, rocket pods, white phosphorus and incendiary bombs, delayed-action incendiary canisters, cluster bombs, and antitank guided missiles.

Good equipment alone, of course, is not sufficient to fulfill the General Staff's vision of the VDV as a group capable of fighting on its own deep in enemy territory. No less important is the caliber of the personnel. The VDV's position as a premier fighting force ensures that airborne units get the cream of Soviet conscripts. Selection is done on the basis of physical stamina and intelligence, plus such factors as Communist party affiliation and previous sport-parachuting experience. Once in the VDV, the men are trained to razor sharpness. Remembers one: "They exhausted us with sprint marches in the middle of the night. The whole day was crammed full with karate, firing practice, parachute jumping, and political training. Frequent nighttime alarm drills forced us to learn how to switch our body clocks and mobilize our internal strength."

The officer corps is forged with particular care. In 1964, the VDV established an Airborne Forces Command School in the city of Ryazan, a ninety-minute train ride southeast of Moscow. Competition to be accepted as a VDV korsant, or officer cadet, is legendary; each year, as many as 32,500 applicants vie for the 500 slots

A New Breed of Soviet Helicopter

The Mi-28 Havoc attack helicopter *(below)*, owes much of its design to losses of Hind helicopters during the war in Afghanistan. This workhorse of the VDV and other Soviet forces served both as an attack helicopter and, with a capacity of eight soldiers, as a troop transport.

The twin-engine Hind is a large target and relatively easy to hit with groundfire. To reduce the risk from heat-seeking surface-to-air missiles such as the Stinger, the Hind has deflectors to dilute engine exhaust with the cooler air of the prop wash. Diverting heat away from the ground conformed to Soviet attack-helicopter practice of the time: a Hind formation circling at 2,000 feet, as individual helicopters peeled off to attack targets.

In Afghanistan, however, the Mujahedin often occupied mountain positions that permitted them to fire on the Hinds from above. Because the engines are mounted close together atop the fuselage, one burst of groundfire could damage both.

To improve survivability, the Havoc was designed smaller than the Hind; it has a crew of two and has no troop-carrying role. Bulletproof glass up to two inches thick and other cockpit armor offer greater protection to the Havoc crew.

The helicopter's twin engines are mounted on opposite sides of the fuselage, widely spaced to reduce the chance of both being knocked out by a single hit. Exhaust deflectors aim the hot gases downward, a change that is more than a concession to mountain warfare. Soviet helicopter pilots are adopting nap-of-the-earth flying for concealment. A hot exhaust plume rising above a hill could give them away.

available. Those chosen tend to be fairly mature—60 percent of them are married by the time they graduate—and they must be willing to accept such un-Russian restrictions as a prohibition on alcohol, even when they are off-duty. During the four-year program, the korsanti take courses that lead to a university-level degree in military engineering. They must endure grueling physical trials—parachute jumps in below-zero temperatures, and twenty-five-mile marches with only a single canteen of water to slake their thirst. Between such tests, they are drilled in every facet of VDV operations, from hand-to-hand combat to vehicle repair. The rewards are significant: In addition to the respect they gain as blue-beret officers, VDV officers—as well as members of the lower ranks—draw more pay than their counterparts in the regular infantry.

Not long after its recasting as a fully mechanized force, the

A bystander displays a bloodied Czechoslovak flag as Soviet paratroopers roll through the streets of Prague riding an ASU-85 assault gun of the VDV. In its first post-World War II deployment, the VDV spearheaded a 1968 invasion to crush Czechoslovakia's "Prague Spring" reform movement.

VDV had occasion to perform a desant that would send shivers throughout the world. The operation, modeled on the airfield attacks in Manchuria more than twenty years earlier, began on the evening of Tuesday, August 20, 1968. At 10:30, the control tower at Ruzyne International Airport in Prague, the capital of Czechoslovakia, picked up a "Mayday" call. A pilot identifying himself as the captain of a Soviet commercial flight was requesting clearance for an emergency landing. He spoke Russian, not English, the universal language of commercial aviation.

This was an anxious time in Prague—especially when it came to the Soviets, overlords of Eastern Europe for two decades. Earlier in the year, the secretary of Czechoslovakia's Communist party, Alexander Dubček, had announced measures designed to reform communism in his nation. He was summoned to Moscow to explain himself, but he refused to go. In response, the Soviet Union, Poland, East Germany, Hungary, and Bulgaria began assembling an invasion force; by August, some 500,000 Warsaw Pact troops stood poised along the Czech borders, awaiting the order to snuff out Dubček's bid for national self-determination.

Hearing Russian from the supposedly distressed Soviet plane, air traffic controllers denied permission to land, directing the aircraft to a nearby military facility. But the plane touched down anyway, and when it pulled up to the terminal, it disgorged a force of Spetsnaz commandos armed with assault rifles. They rushed to the control tower and took it over. Then Soviet MiG-21 fighters began buzzing the airport, providing cover as two military transports landed. From their ample bellies scrambled paratroopers of the Vozdushno-Desantnyye Voiska's 103d Guards Airborne Division, garrisoned in the Belorussian city of Vitebsk, about 900 miles distant. These well-rehearsed troops quickly secured the administration buildings and all roads leading into and out of the airport. At that point, larger Soviet transports began landing and unloading ASU-85 self-propelled artillery. VDV forces mounted up and, in the dead of night, roared into Prague and took control of undefended government offices and communications facilities.

By morning, Czechoslovakia was firmly under Soviet control. The massed Warsaw Pact forces that crossed the borders by land met little resistance, which was just as well for them. Analyzing the floundering performance of the armored columns sent to suppress the politically wayward Czechs, one Western observer wrote, "The airborne element was the only part of the operation which could have been claimed to be a success."

The efficiency of the Prague desant earned the admiration of Soviet leaders as well, and when another political threat flared up eleven years later, they arranged a replay. This time the scene was Afghanistan, an Islamic nation on the USSR's southern border.

Afghanistan is a Texas-size country with a population in the late 1960s of some 14 million. Sectored by high mountain ranges, further divided by tribal passions, sorely lacking in basic industries and communications, it was a land largely bypassed by the twentieth century. Moscow had provided the government in Kabul with military and economic aid since the mid-1950s, but Afghanistan was among the politically wobbliest of the Soviet client states. In April 1978, a coup brought to power an obscure leftist named Noor Muhammad Taraki, who soon spelled out his party's agenda: "We want to clean Islam in Afghanistan of the ballast and dirt of bad traditions, superstition, and erroneous belief." Toward that end, Taraki decreed more equality for Afghanistan's historically suppressed women, land reform, forgiveness of taxes owed by peasants, and a redesigned national flag that was completely red. It had not a trace of green, the traditional Islamic color.

Though Taraki's reforms were populist in nature, the "bad traditions" they replaced had lain at the foundation of Afghan society, which was deeply conservative in both religion and politics. All across the nation, Afghans organized resistance groups, and by the end of 1978, the rebels were at war with the army of the Democratic Republic of Afghanistan (DRA) in many provinces. In March 1979, Taraki ordered a DRA army division into the western city of Herāt to suppress a demonstration. Instead of doing so, however, most of the troops deserted to join the opposition, going so far as to loot their arsenals and turn modern weapons over to rebel leaders. Soon, angry mobs were roaming through Herāt unchecked. Among their targets were Soviet advisers and their families. As many as 200 Soviet men, women, and children were hacked to death, and pieces of their corpses were triumphantly paraded through the city. The situation took another turn in September, when Taraki was overthrown and ordered killed by a rival named Hafizullah Amin. A cosmopolitan man (he had learned English during studies at Columbia University and the University of Wisconsin), Amin instantly aroused Soviet suspicion. A KGB major who later defected recalled that "our investigations showed Amin to be a smooth-talking fascist who was secretly pro-Western. We suspected that he had links with the CIA." Soviet president Leonid Brezhnev decided to replace Amin with an official more compliant to Moscow: Babrak Karmal, then serving as Afghan ambassador to Czechoslovakia. An invasion would be necessary to bring this about.

As autumn turned to winter, several VDV regiments were flown into Kabul, along with their BMD fighting vehicles, ostensibly to help the DRA deal with Mujahedin attacks on the city and on a major air base at Bagram, forty miles away. In mid-December, a VDV detachment sent to Bagram went north to secure the Salang Pass, the route to Afghanistan from the Soviet Central Asia republic of Turkmenistan. On December 26, 1979, VDV units—which had been waiting tensely for two weeks at air bases throughout the Soviet Union—were ordered into their transports and flown to Kabul. They intended to waste no time fastening their grip on the city. "We started up the BMDs while we were still in the air," remembered one of them. "The wheels of the plane had just touched the ground when the crew released the door and lowered the ramp, and we drove out the vehicles. The airplanes immediately took off and returned home for another shipment."

During the airlift, Soviet Air Force and Aeroflot planes made 280 flights to bring in elements of the 105th Guards Airborne Division. These units fanned through Kabul to seize key points. Meanwhile, numbers of Spetsnaz surrounded Tajbeg Palace, where Amin had retreated. There they killed him.

An hour later, a broadcast in the voice of Kabul Radio announced that Babrak Karmal had assumed control of the country and was now requesting Soviet aid to restore order. This message was particularly surprising to the Afghan staff of Kabul Radio, which still clung to control of the studio and transmitter. In fact, Karmal had not yet arrived in the capital, and nearly 20,000 of the Soviet troops he was just now seeming to request were already in Afghanistan. The broadcast was actually a clever subterfuge transmitted from the Soviet city of Termez.

Four days later, no doubt encouraged by the swift success of the VDV desant, Soviet leader Leonid Brezhnev sent the newly installed Karmal a congratulatory New Year's Eve message expressing confidence in his ability to defend "the sovereignty, independence, and national dignity of the new Afghanistan." But the Afghan people had radically different notions about the meaning of these words. The Mujahedin were ready and willing to take on the invaders from the north, no matter how many troops and advanced weapons Moscow shipped to Kabul.

"War in Afghanistan," said one top Soviet commander, "is very strange." In the light of past conflicts, including World War II, that was perhaps an understatement. The contest in Afghanistan was a piecemeal war, fought against a fragmented, ill-defined enemy. The population was divided into many ethnic and religious groups, fiercely loyal to their own traditions, and the resistance movement mirrored this disunity: The Mujahedin followed the orders of local leaders, who rarely cooperated with one another.

Soviet military planners never hoped to defeat the Mujahedin by taking and controlling territory. Their strategy was more fundamental. They sought to deprive the guerrillas of their base of support by terrorizing the people, bombing villages, destroying irrigation systems and crops, and scattering huge numbers of antipersonnel mines over the countryside. In consequence, a substantial portion of the Afghan population would flee—more than two million to refugee camps in Pakistan, a million to Iran.

The war was largely defined by terrain. Soviet forces intended chiefly for combat on the plains of Europe found themselves fighting in a landscape of almost unrelieved ruggedness. Afghanistan completely lacked a rail network and possessed only a few paved roads. The poor transportation system made any movement of men or matériel on the ground a perilous affair. Convoys forced to crawl across mountain passes or through steep-sided valleys were vulnerable to ambush—a sudden hail of fire from the an-

Vanguard of the December 1979 invasion of Afghanistan, the 105th Guards Airborne Division deploys on the outskirts of Kabul. The mass of vehicles exemplifies the Soviet doctrine of total mechanization of airborne forces.

cient but accurate Lee-Enfield rifles that many of the guerrillas carried, or a bludgeoning by mortars or Chinese-made 107-mm rockets—or even a landslide launched by Mujahedin lurking on the mountainsides. After an attack, the rebels had an infinity of hiding places to choose from, slipping away to caves in the mountains or bases in remote valleys tucked among the peaks.

Initially, the Soviets and troops loyal to the government tried to fight the war with conventional ground forces, but tanks and other heavy weapons were of limited value against the elusive guerrillas. Ambushes took a dreadful toll in the mountains, not only because movement was slow and restricted but also because the radio communication was poor and units often lost contact with one another. After the first year of the war, the Soviet military leaders turned increasingly to their airborne force. Although the VDV used BMD fighting vehicles and other light armor for ground combat, the paratroops moved about primarily by helicopter, following the American model in Vietnam.

A key role of the sky soldiers was to protect truck convoys. Transport helicopters landed detachments on the heights overlooking the route as a convoy approached, then lifted them out and repositioned them farther ahead when the trucks had gone by. Meanwhile, Hind gunships lingered over the convoy or blasted away at suspected ambush positions. Despite such measures, big losses occurred—sometimes self-inflicted. In June 1981, guerrillas ambushed a 120-truck convoy at a chokepoint on the road running from the Salang Pass to Kabul. When it became clear that valuable matériel was about to fall into rebel hands, the Soviets blew up most of the trucks and evacuated their crews by helicopter and armored vehicle.

Although Soviet forces frequently found themselves fighting for their lives, they also visited terrible punishment on the Mujahedin and their supporters. A VDV sergeant described how a major encounter might go: "Usually in the case of an outstanding resistance, several echelons had to participate in a battle. First Su-25 jets bombed and strafed the area. After that, helicopter gunships blasted the mountains with rocket fire, with one of them attacking, the others covering. Then the artillery got their turn. Finally the soldiers went in for the finishing touch, destroying huts, crops, fighting with those who remained alive."

Soviet troops called the Mujahedin *dushmani* (bandits) or *dukshi* (ghosts), in recognition of their skill at appearing from nowhere and

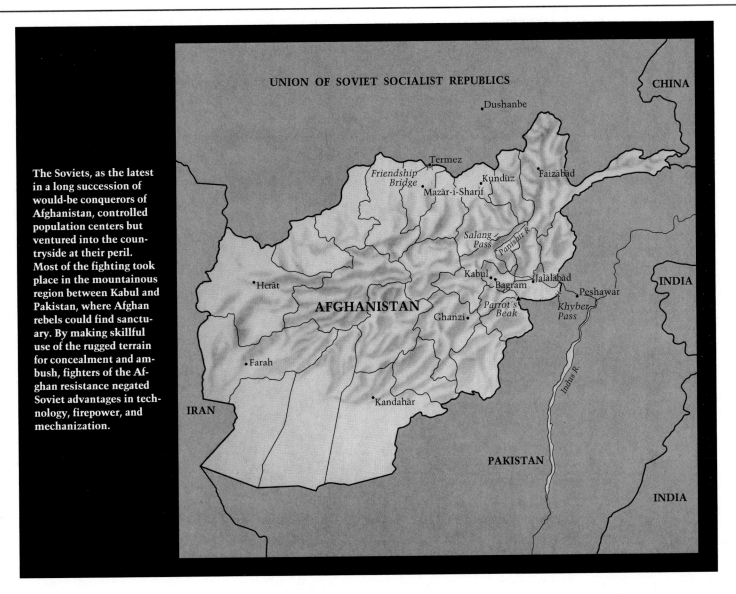

The Soviets, as the latest in a long succession of would-be conquerors of Afghanistan, controlled population centers but ventured into the countryside at their peril. Most of the fighting took place in the mountainous region between Kabul and Pakistan, where Afghan rebels could find sanctuary. By making skillful use of the rugged terrain for concealment and ambush, fighters of the Afghan resistance negated Soviet advantages in technology, firepower, and mechanization.

then fading back into the landscape when their attack was over. One VDV paratrooper recalled the deadly surprise sprung after his unit entered a deserted village. Patrols were sent out and guards posted, but to no avail. At some time in the past, for an unknown reason, "an underground tunnel had been dug from this nameless village to the mountains. Now the dushmani were using it. At night, they secretly crawled to the surface behind the mosque and butchered fourteen men who were sleeping in a hut. Then they went away just as quietly."

A Vozdushno-Desantnyye Voiska scouting party dismounts from an Mi-17 Hip helicopter during an operation in the Panjshir Valley in July of 1985. Shortly after this photograph was taken, the men came under fire from Mujahedin rebels as they scrambled up the barren slope. The VDV's usual practice for heliborne insertions was to send four or five advance teams such as this one ahead of the main body to secure the landing zone.

Another paratrooper remembered: "When we arrived, the commander gave us one simple piece of advice. 'The territory of our base is our territory. Anywhere else is dangerous; you could easily die. Therefore always be vigilant.' I've never forgotten those words." Peril lay behind every boulder, even close to the center of Soviet and governmental power. Late in the war, said the paratrooper, "we didn't go out on missions but occupied the hills and low mountains surrounding Kabul. Our job was to make sure that no guerrillas moved through the area or attempted to take up positions in the mountains. At night, the sentries were ordered to shoot at anyone or anything after asking 'Who goes there?' Sometimes it was a guerrilla, sometimes an animal, sometimes just the wind."

Some of the heaviest fighting took place in the Panjshir Valley, north of Kabul. Bounded by soaring peaks and cleaved by winding valleys that offered hiding places and escape routes, the Panjshir was controlled by the most able of all Mujahedin leaders, Ahmad Shah Masoud. A former engineering student, Masoud was well versed in the literature of guerrilla warfare and a decisive, canny commander. Some 3,000 men served in his army of irregulars, and they harried convoys on the Salang-to-Kabul road without mercy.

In the spring of 1982, Masoud's forces ventured south to strike the military air base at Bagram, where they destroyed several MiG-21s. The Soviets responded by staging their largest operation to date. On May 10, attack aircraft began an intensive aerial bombardment to soften up the valley, which by then had lost almost half of its prewar population of 80,000. A week later, a regiment of the 103d Guards Airborne Division deployed by helicopter deep into the Panjshir, the first thrust of a three-pronged attack. In short order, Soviet and DRA mechanized columns muscled into the valley from both ends in an effort to drive the Mujahedin toward the paratroops. But even with a combined force of at least 15,000 men enjoying close air support from Hind gunships, the Soviets and Afghans did not have an easy time of it against Masoud's rebels. Only after two weeks of savage fighting—battles that resulted in 80 percent of the Panjshir villages razed and perhaps 1,200 civilians killed—did the Mujahedin retreat, having lost about 100 men. Soviet losses were four times greater. A private wrote home about his company: "There's practically nothing left. They're all either in coffins or in the hospital." Less than a month after VDV paratroops went in, the Soviets withdrew most of their forces. Soon afterward, Masoud and his rebels came down from the mountains and reclaimed the valley.

In April 1984, the Soviets made another attempt to defeat Masoud. This effort featured two significant changes in tactics. The first was carpet bombing from high altitude. The bombs exploded without warning, a demoralizing experience for the victims who survived. With the rebel forces now grown to 5,000, the Soviets called in thirty-six Tu-16 bombers and dozens of Su-24 fighter-bombers from bases on their own side of the border. The bombardment lifted after one day to allow some 15,000 Soviet troops to pour into the Panjshir, with helicopters bringing in BMD fighting vehicles and artillery.

Ten days later, the Soviets sprang their second surprise. Aware that the Mujahedin routinely retreated through the high passes of the tributary valleys, the Soviet command inserted VDV elements by helicopter to block key routes. Simultaneously, the troops on the floor of the Panjshir began driving the rebels up into the mountains.

It was an appallingly difficult campaign. At one point, three companies were marching along the banks of the Panjshir River. They had been told that Soviet troops controlled the ridges above them—but that information was wrong. Artyom Borovik, a Soviet journalist, reported what happened. "The men had quickly grown tired in the stifling heat. The commander of the battalion ordered them to stop for a cigarette break. They sank to the hot ground, propping themselves up against their backpacks. The silence was punctuated only by the clanging of submachine guns and the striking of matches. The aroma of cigarette smoke spread through the air."

Without warning, this peaceful interlude was rent by the crack of rifles and whine of bullets ricocheting from the rocks as the Mujahedin opened fire from three different directions. "The commander of the battalion barely had time to scream 'R-a-a-a-i-d!' " said Borovik, "before a bullet hit him in the forehead. He fell back-first into the river." Seventy soldiers died with him.

But the Mujahedin losses were heavy as well, and several rebel leaders were captured. After the operation, the Soviet and DRA forces built forts in the lower part of the valley, curbing Masoud's freedom of movement.

By then, however, prospects for defeating the Mujahedin were

An Afghan rebel turns a Soviet SA-7 surface-to-air missile against its makers. The Mujahedin acquired sophisticated Soviet weaponry by ambushing convoys and also from such diverse sources as the Palestine Liberation Organization and even the CIA. Though later supplanted by the American Stinger and British Blowpipe missiles, the SA-7 nevertheless proved effective in the early years of the war against Soviet helicopters.

dimming. An early symptom of the Soviet military dilemma was the changing flight pattern of their Hind attack helicopters—the weapons that the Mujahedin dreaded most. At the start of the war, the gunships were used in groups of four to eight, circling over the battleground in leisurely fashion and then, one by one, diving down to blaze away with their machine guns and rockets. But the Mujahedin were not without defenses; deserters from the DRA army provided them with Soviet-made shoulder-fired heat-seeking surface-to-air missiles. As the missiles began to take a toll, Hind pilots responded with low-level approaches and a variety of maneuvers that made their gunships hard to hit; they also ejected flares to decoy the missiles away. Yet losses not only continued but began to reach unsustainable levels when visually guided British Blowpipe missiles and heat-seeking American Stingers came to the Mujahedin in 1986. The Stinger was particularly lethal. Shoulder-fired like the SA-7 and the Blowpipe, it had a highly sensitive infrared seeker in its nose and, traveling faster than the speed of sound, could hit a target at a range of one and a half miles. Kill rates exceeding 50 percent were reported—most likely an exaggeration, but nonetheless suggestive of the value of the missile. Masoud himself said: "There are only two things Afghans must have: the Koran and Stingers." The guerrillas obtained many hundreds of them covertly from the United States, and they contributed mightily to the destruction of Soviet planes during the war. About 1,000 aircraft were lost in all; an estimated 80 percent of them were helicopters.

As the struggle for Afghanistan wore on, seeming ever more futile and violent, morale in the Soviet ranks slumped. Soviet soldiers, like their American counterparts in Vietnam, discovered the dangerous solace of drugs, easier to get in a Muslim nation than alcohol. For the most part, said a defector, the troops "smoke hashish and cocaine. They get hold of them by means of sale and exchange. They sell literally everything possible, even arms and ammunition."

In 1989, the Soviet Union—now led by the reform-minded Mikhail Gorbachev—finally called it quits and turned the prosecution of the war over to the Kabul government. Much of the Soviet equipment, including many of the VDV fighting vehicles that had proved of such limited use in the wilds of Afghanistan, was handed to the DRA army. The last of the Soviet forces crossed from Afghanistan into Turkmenistan in mid-February. The nine-year misadventure had cost 13,833 Soviet lives.

Standards flying, a column of BTR-70 armored personnel carriers, loaded with smiling VDV soldiers, returns from the Afghan war across the Friendship Bridge. Built before the conflict, the trestle spans the Amu-Darya River, on the Soviet border.

It had also created heroes, and most of them were men of the Vozdushno-Desantnyye Voiska or the helicopter crews that worked with them. Upward of half the coveted Hero of the Soviet Union medals awarded for actions in Afghanistan went to these forces.

By the time of the withdrawal, the VDV was working hard to address deficiencies and enhance its fighting abilities in future wars. Some of its self-examination focused on reviving the original operational mode of an airborne force—parachuting from a plane. There is little subterfuge in a conventional airdrop; ground defenses can hear the transports arrive overhead to disgorge their human cargo. Seeking to shield paratroopers from landing-zone groundfire, the Soviets were adapting an advance made by sport parachutists— the glide parachute. In the late 1980s, such canopies had a glide ratio of three to one, meaning that a paratrooper could maneuver one yard horizontally for every foot of descent. In theory, an assault force equipped with parachutes having even higher glide ratios could be dropped as far as twenty-five miles from its target, enabling it to reach the landing zone in virtual secrecy.

As an alternative, the Soviets are investigating the use of American-made microlight aircraft as stealthy penetration platforms. Microlights—30-mile-per-hour single-passenger planes built like hang gliders—can be surprisingly quiet and are difficult to detect with radar.

However they get there, the troops on the ground will be able to count on improved air support. During the 1980s, the Soviets unveiled three new helicopters: the Ka-36/136 Hokum, an experimental model thought to be designed specifically for shooting down other helicopters; the Mi-28 Havoc, a tactical helicopter smaller and more maneuverable than the Hind but possessing substantially greater firepower; and the Mi-32, a transport with about a third the capacity but more than twice the speed of the Mi-17 Hip it will replace.

As for manpower, Moscow seems intent on preserving the three-to-one advantage that its air-assault arm has traditionally enjoyed over the similar forces of the United States. In strength as well as skill, the Vozdushno-Desantnyye Voiska will retain the status it has long held among the world's sky soldiers: an instrument of stunning power and unique capabilities. ★

Foreign Legion to the Rescue

On May 17, 1978, at ten o'clock in the morning, the telephone rang in the office of Colonel Philippe Erulin, commanding officer of the Deuxième Régiment Étranger de Parachutistes (Two REP for short). Without preface or explanation, he was instructed to have his unit—the only airdrop-qualified component of the French Foreign Legion—packed and prepared to deploy in six hours.

Erulin immediately set about mobilizing the regiment. Soldiers on leave or detached from normal duties at Two REP's base of operations at Calvi, Corsica, were hastily recalled. The men began collecting and checking their battle gear. Four hours past the unrealistically short deadline,

the colonel could report that his paratroops were ready for action, and by early the next morning, they had reached Solenzara Air Force Base on the other side of the island. No one in the unit, not even Colonel Erulin, knew their destination or mission. The uncertainty mattered little to the legionnaires of Two REP; as an elite and integral component of France's rapid reaction force, the regiment had to be ready for battle anywhere, at any time.

As military organizations go, the French Foreign Legion is unique. Commanded by French officers, the legion comprises men of all nationalities, many of whom have a past they would rather not discuss. Their training is harsh and their reputation is fearsome. The parachute regiment is the cream of the legion.

At Solenzara, the reason for urgency was revealed: A bloodbath was feared under way in far-off Zaire, more than 3,000 miles from Two REP's base in Corsica. Formerly called the Belgian Congo, Zaire, like many African countries encompassing a multitude of ethnic groups, had been held together more by colonial rule than by any sense of nationhood. Belgium had educated the Congo's disparate tribes in a common tongue, French, which remained the official language of Zaire.

The country's postindependence history had been one

The sky behind Kolwezi's Impala Hotel blossoms with the parachutes of the Second Parachute Regiment, French Foreign Legion. Many Western residents of the town were murdered in the hotel before the legion arrived.

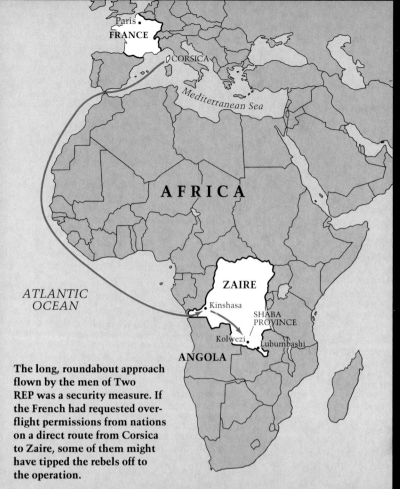

The long, roundabout approach flown by the men of Two REP was a security measure. If the French had requested over-flight permissions from nations on a direct route from Corsica to Zaire, some of them might have tipped the rebels off to the operation.

prolonged power struggle between rival factions. For ex-ample, the southern province of Shaba, rich in copper and far removed from the capital of Kinshasa, had experienced a bloody attempt at secession by Marxists in 1977. Zaire's president, Mobutu Sese Seku, had put down the revolt and driven the separatists out of Shaba and into the neighbor-ing country of Angola. The sympathetic government trained and equipped them to carry on the fight as the Congolese National Liberation Front—known by its French initials, FNLC.

Now, some 4,000 of these rebels returned to Shaba in a renewed bid for independence. Most of Mobutu's troops in the vicinity, loyal but poorly trained, fled, and the FNLC troops quickly captured the mining town of Kolwezi, though government forces held onto the airport three miles away. The Zairian Army tried a parachute drop on the town in company strength, but the rebels were waiting and killed many of the soldiers as they floated to earth in their parachutes, then quickly dispatched the rest when they hit the ground.

At first, the FNLC's occupation of Kolwezi had been orderly, but discipline among the irregulars soon broke down. A chaos of looting ensued. Rapists and murderers

Troops of the first wave in Kinshasa strug-gle to attach their equipment bags to U.S. T-10 parachutes procured from Zaire.

terrorized the city's black residents and 3,000 white expatriates, most of whom were French or Belgians involved with Gecamines, a copper-mining concern. An immediate rescue operation was deemed critical to prevent a wholesale massacre.

President Mobutu asked the French government for assistance. Concerned for the safety of Zaire's many French residents, President Valéry Giscard d'Estaing agreed that France would undertake the mission—code-named Operation Leopard. President Jimmy Carter, meanwhile, offered American logistical support.

Apprised of the situation in Kolwezi, Colonel Erulin faced a daunting task. Simultaneously, he had to devise and implement a plan to transport his regiment to a staging point in Zaire, then get his men into Kolwezi as a cohesive force while maintaining the element of surprise.

Obstacles began to appear immediately. Five Air France DC-8 airliners were on hand at Solenzara, but they were sufficient to carry only two-thirds of the troops and none of Two REP's vehicles. So Erulin had to divide his regiment into two contingents. Four rifle companies, the mortar and reconnaissance platoons, and part of the headquarters company—650 men in all—boarded the planes for the ten-hour flight to Kinshasa. To make matters worse, space limitations aboard the DC-8s forced the first contingent to leave their parachute packs behind; they would draw chutes from the Zairian Army upon arrival in Kinshasa. The troops left behind at Solenzara, along with all the regiment's vehicles, would follow in U.S. Air Force C-5 and C-141 transports and fly directly to Lubumbashi, capital of Shaba Province and 160 miles from Kolwezi.

By 11:30 that night, Erulin and his advance group were on the tarmac at Kinshasa airport, grappling with preparations for the assault on Kolwezi. The colonel believed that if the rebels got wind of a rescue operation, they would certainly begin mass executions. He therefore decided against landing his men at the airport and marching the three miles to Kolwezi. Instead, he would conduct an airdrop right on the town—a much more hazardous proposition—and hope to surprise the FNLC troops.

As the urgency of the situation increased, delays multiplied. French equipment bags, in which Two REP para-

A Zairian Air Force C-130 discharges its load of paratroops over DZ Alpha *(right),* who, upon hitting the ground, move quickly to gather up their billowing chutes. Fortunately for Two REP, rebel resistance near the DZ was minimal.

did not fit the American parachutes supplied by Zaire. The men, sweltering in the heat and high humidity, and bleary-eyed from lack of sleep, had to jury-rig their combat gear to the American harnesses with rope and wire. Two of Zaire's C-130 Hercules transports were grounded with mechanical difficulties, leaving four C-130s and two smaller French Air Force C-160 Transalls for the jump. The reduced number of aircraft compelled Erulin to split his regiment a second time, forming two waves that, in the absence of additional aircraft, would reach Kolwezi at least nine hours apart. To get as much firepower as possible, the colonel wanted three companies of troops on the ground in the first wave. To get them, he crammed eighty paratroops into planes that were meant to carry sixty-five.

Kolwezi is divided into Old Town, with a mostly African population, and New Town, a little to the north and east, where the majority of the Europeans resided. Erulin had no current information about the state of affairs in Kolwezi, but earlier reports indicated the rebels were holding hostages in both sections of Kolwezi.

Working with detailed maps, Erulin marked his drop zones. He chose an open area—designated DZ Alpha—just north of Old Town for the first contingent. From there they could fan out, occupy blocking positions along a main road connecting the old and new parts of town, and begin a search for hostages. Another landing site, DZ Bravo, was outlined to the east, on the other side of New Town. Depending on the situation, Erulin thought to land the second wave there.

After a pause for fog to clear, the six transports took to the air for the bumpy, four-and-a-half-hour flight to Kolwezi. It was sheer misery for the three companies of thoroughly exhausted men packed in shoulder to shoulder.

After making one pass over Kolwezi to identify the drop zone, the planes lowered their rear cargo ramps, and the paratroopers—not knowing what sort of reception awaited them—stepped into space, fifty-three hours after the telephone call to their colonel and more than 3,000 miles from home.

In a mission pervaded with problems, luck finally smiled on Two REP. It became evident at once that Erulin's men had achieved the most crucial element of Operation Leopard, tactical surprise. The assault from the

Having cleared Kolwezi of FNLC rebels, Two REP troopers, directed by Colonel Erulin (inset, foreground), fan out into the bush searching for rebel strongholds on the second day of Operation Leopard.

air caught the rebels off guard, and the jumpers met only sporadic fire as they descended. The only casualties resulted from landings: four fractures and two sprains.

The three companies of the first wave assembled and went into action fifteen minutes after hitting the ground. One company took up a position near the railway station, astride the road connecting Old Town and New Town. A second moved southwest toward the hospital in Old Town and the headquarters of the mining firm outside Kolwezi, while the third moved directly south into Old Town, trying to reach a school where it was thought hostages were being held. As each element advanced, the legionnaires saw why their presence was so urgently needed. The rotting corpses of blacks and whites, some half-eaten by dogs, were strewn everywhere. Many were horribly mutilated. The sight filled the paratroops with grim determination.

Advancing house by house through the streets of Old Town, Erulin's men managed to reach the school, where a hundred hostages were discovered in the basement. Thirty-five more hostages were freed when the paratroops stormed the police station and killed the rebel guards.

The Two REP jumpers had expected to encounter nothing more than irregular infantry, but the FNLC rebels had a surprise in store. One legion squad leader recalled he had set up a roadblock on a railway overpass when suddenly, "to our front, gears grinding, appeared the first of three armored cars." The lead vehicle slowed to take a corner, then headed straight for the sergeant's position at high speed. His squad had only two portable antitank rockets. By the time he and another trooper had loaded the launcher, the first armored car was only fifty yards away, with an antitank rocket aimed straight ahead. The sergeant recalled what happened next:

" 'Nom de Dieu,' I yelled, 'fire, fire!' CRASH! The launcher barked and the rocket smacked into the vehicle's turret. Its driver, dead, fell out of the side door." At the sight of this, the other two armored cars quickly reversed direction and sped away.

By sunset, the paratroops had secured Old Town. At this juncture, the second wave in their transports arrived over Kolwezi. With darkness falling and the situation on the ground still confused, Colonel Erulin called off the jump, ordering the planes to return the following morning.

Arms at the ready, legionnaires move briskly through the New Town section of Kolwezi, breaking down doors in a house-to-house search for rebels and European hostages. This kind of sweep is among the most nerve-racking forms of combat; any door could hide an ambush.

For the legionnaires on the ground, the struggle continued through the night. Brief but intense firefights flared up in the dark as the troops discovered and routed isolated pockets of rebels. With no sleep for three days, Two REP was counting on adrenaline and Dexedrine to keep going.

At dawn on May 20, the second wave returned. The rebels seemed as surprised by this second jump as by the first. Erulin ordered the mortar and reconnaissance platoons to use DZ Alpha but directed the fourth rifle company to DZ Bravo. Moving in from an unexpected direction, this unit was able to capture New Town in a matter of hours.

With the built-up areas of Kolwezi secure, Two REP fanned out into the bush looking for more rebels and hostages. The fiercest resistance was encountered near a mining facility three miles northwest of New Town. The legionnaires were pinned down until the mortar platoon was brought up to lay a barrage on the position, which was finally taken around sundown. The rebels suffered eighty dead in this pitched battle, while the paratroops lost four killed.

Meanwhile, Two REP's vehicles had been driven the ten hours from Lubumbashi. They facilitated mopping-up operations that would occupy the regiment for the next week. At that time, Kolwezi was turned over to a multinational, African peacekeeping force, and Two REP returned to Corsica aboard American C-141 transports.

Operation Leopard was judged a complete success and stands as a prime example of what a small, highly trained and motivated elite unit can accomplish in the face of a numerically superior enemy. Given the extemporaneous nature of the mission and the plague of logistical problems, it is remarkable that Two REP achieved such a stunning victory. At a cost of 5 dead and 25 wounded, the regiment had killed 250 FNLC rebels and captured large stocks of weapons. And although 120 expatriates had died in the orgy of violence, the legionnaires had undoubtedly saved the rest.

A legionnaire warily guards three unarmed suspects emerging from the bush.
By this point in Operation Leopard,
most rebels had fled back to their bases
in Angola. Interrogation of these men revealed that they were Zairian soldiers.

4

Red Berets in the Falklands

Men of Britain's Third Parachute Battalion—Three Para—set out for their next objective after capturing Mount Longdon in the 1982 Falklands War against Argentina. The sky soldiers' ability to hike long distances under miserable conditions proved as important to winning the war as their fighting qualities.

Writing about the Falkland Islands in 1770, Samuel Johnson, England's great man of letters, advised that it was a place "thrown aside from human use, stormy in winter, barren in summer, an island which not even the southern savages have dignified with habitation, where a garrison must be kept in a state that contemplates with envy the exiles of Siberia." Dr. Johnson had never personally set foot on the small British colony in the lower latitudes of the South Atlantic, 400 miles off the coast of today's Argentina. But he had ample testimony upon which to base an opinion. "I tarry in this miserable desert, suffering everything for the love of God," wrote the priest ministering to a small band of colonists at the time. And a British soldier serving in the settlement heartily echoed those sentiments. The Falklands, he said, were "the most detestable place I was ever at in all my life."

Yet it has been the fate of these forlorn flyspecks to be the objects of acrimonious dispute almost from the day in 1690 when Captain John Strong went ashore, named the place after the First Lord of the Admiralty, Lord Falkland, and then sailed on. The contestants for the boggy, treeless, savagely wind-swept islands initially were England and Spain, then England and Argentina.

Continuous British occupation dates to 1833, when an expeditionary force ejected a few Argentine gauchos at gunpoint. In time, the islands became home to about 1,800 inhabitants who made a living from the sheep that outnumbered them 300 to 1. But Argentina never gave up its claim, and in 1982 the simmering resentment was brought to a boil by a military junta eager to use the Malvinas, as they were known to Argentines, to divert attention from its own shaky political grasp and the country's massive economic problems. The British, meanwhile, stood firm in their longtime occupancy and on the right of the islanders—most of whom considered themselves British subjects—to political self-determination.

So it was that on April 2, 1982, a heavily armed Argentine invasion force landed in the Falklands, overwhelmed a handful of Royal Marines, and forced them to lie facedown on the ground as prisoners. In London, immediately upon learning of this affront, Prime Minister Margaret Thatcher told a tumultuous House of Commons that her majesty's government was determined "to see the islands returned to British administration"—by whatever means necessary. The short, fierce Falklands War was on.

It would be a conflict in which Britain would swiftly mobilize its military assets and thrust an armada of more than a hundred vessels and 29,000 soldiers, sailors, and aviators 8,000 miles into the South Atlantic. To face them, the Argentine junta would pour troops into the Falklands until there were 11,000 heavily armed, well-dug-in defenders. They would outweigh the British infantry component by more than two to one—the very reverse of accepted doctrine, which postulates a three-to-one numerical edge of attackers over defenders. Yet in the event, the Argentines would find themselves overmatched. For among the ships and planes, the marines and sailors, the pilots and commandos sent to win back the Falklands were two battalions of paratroopers—Two Para and Three Para, 1,200 men in all. They were the cream of the British Army, and it was these superbly trained, supremely motivated sky soldiers, arriving by sea and fighting as ordinary foot soldiers, who would devastate the enemy in a series of actions to honor any set of regimental colors.

To many Britons—both civilian and military—fighting seemed unlikely at the start. All agreed that the prime minister's dispatch of a fleet would call the Argentine bluff and that the issue would be resolved diplomatically. But Lieutenant Colonel Hew Pike, commander of Three Para, strongly demurred. Soon after learning that his battalion would accompany the Falklands expedition as part of Three Commando Brigade, Pike told his assembled men that "it seemed very clear that we were likely to fight. I felt that we were very fortunate, and said so."

Less than a week later, on Good Friday, April 9, Pike's battalion sailed from Southampton aboard the luxury liner *Canberra*, which had been commandeered for the emergency. On May 6, they were joined at Ascension Island, midway between the British Isles and the Falklands, by Two Para. This battalion had been recalled to England from an undemanding tour of duty in Belize (formerly Brit-

Stepping from a landing craft into the icy waters at Port San Carlos, an antitank platoon of Three Para begins the tough campaign across East Falkland Island with wet feet. The soldier in the foreground carries a fifty-pound British-made Blowpipe antiaircraft missile launcher. The weapon, used by each side in the Falklands War, was a disappointment, bringing down few of the planes it was fired at.

ish Honduras), which was threatened by a leftist government in its Central American neighbor, Guatemala. In command of Two Para was Lieutenant Colonel Herbert "H" Jones, an ardent officer whose highest ambition was to lead Two Para in battle.

After taking on supplies at Ascension, the British fleet arrived at the Falklands on May 20 and started debarking early the next morning in the vicinity of San Carlos on East Falkland. There was no opposition, and none had been expected. Special operations reconnaissance teams, landed earlier, had reported no enemy positions defending the beach. A prewar Argentine naval study had concluded that San Carlos offered no chance for a successful invasion; the small settlement was, after all, at the opposite end of the island from Stanley, the capital, and between the two stretched fifty miles of seemingly impassable terrain. The Argentine commander, Major General Mario Menendez, had dismissed as a diversion the British ships reported steaming in the direction of San Carlos and was flabbergasted to learn that troops were coming ashore.

The paras and marine commandos suffered their share of mishaps going ashore. Landing craft took longer than expected to load as the

95

The map of East Falkland at right shows the routes of Two Para *(red)* and Three Para *(blue)* across the island from the Port San Carlos area to Stanley. Enlarged areas below and on the facing page highlight actions against Argentine troops.

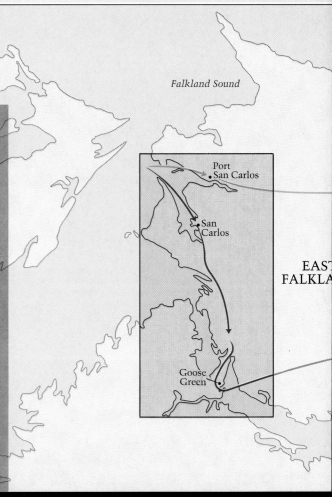

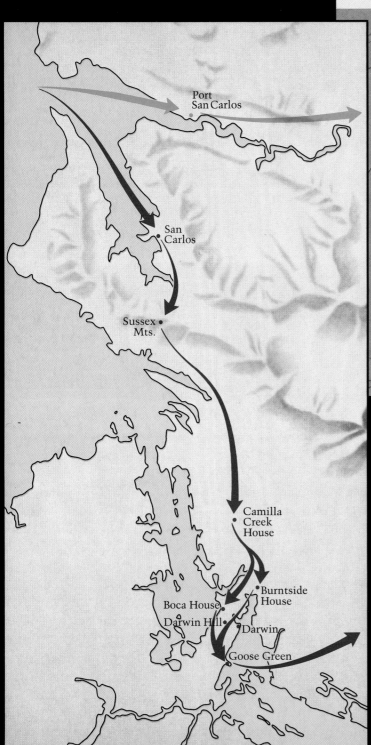

After landing unopposed at Port San Carlos on May 21, 1982, Three Para remained in the area until May 27, when it began an eastern trek across the north side of East Falkland. Meanwhile, Two Para immediately headed south to engage the Argentine garrison at Goose Green, proceeding by way of the Sussex Mountains and Camilla Creek house, where Two Para split up for a two-pronged attack on Goose Green. B Company kept to the west, advancing on Goose Green after a battle at Boca house that lasted several hours. A Company kept to the east. After a firefight with a small Argentine force at Burntside house, the paras approached Goose Green over Darwin Hill, where Colonel "H" Jones, the Two Para commander, was killed leading his men forward. With Darwin Hill taken, the settlement of Darwin capitulated on May 28. Next day, Goose Green gave up without a fight.

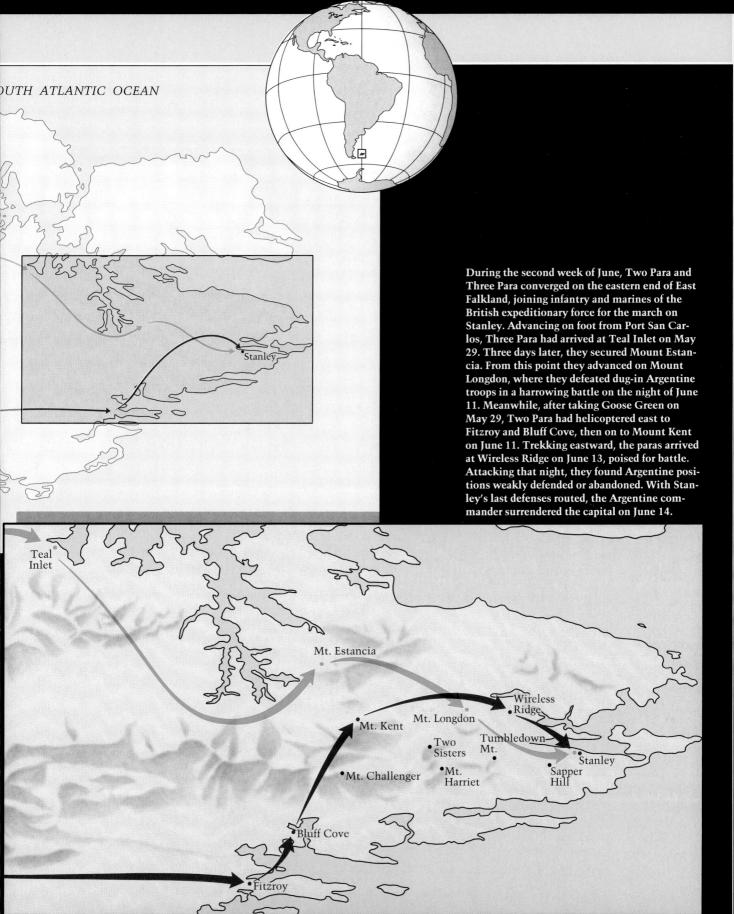

SOUTH ATLANTIC OCEAN

Stanley

During the second week of June, Two Para and Three Para converged on the eastern end of East Falkland, joining infantry and marines of the British expeditionary force for the march on Stanley. Advancing on foot from Port San Carlos, Three Para had arrived at Teal Inlet on May 29. Three days later, they secured Mount Estancia. From this point they advanced on Mount Longdon, where they defeated dug-in Argentine troops in a harrowing battle on the night of June 11. Meanwhile, after taking Goose Green on May 29, Two Para had helicoptered east to Fitzroy and Bluff Cove, then on to Mount Kent on June 11. Trekking eastward, the paras arrived at Wireless Ridge on June 13, poised for battle. Attacking that night, they found Argentine positions weakly defended or abandoned. With Stanley's last defenses routed, the Argentine commander surrendered the capital on June 14.

Teal Inlet

Mt. Estancia

Wireless Ridge

Mt. Kent

Mt. Longdon

Tumbledown Mt.

Two Sisters

Stanley

Mt. Challenger

Mt. Harriet

Sapper Hill

Bluff Cove

Fitzroy

men staggered under the 120-pound weight of their weapons and bergens, or rucksacks, crammed with sleeping bags, arctic clothing, rations, and other gear. The process was further delayed when a Two Para soldier fell into the water between a landing craft and the troopship, suffering a crushed pelvis as the two vessels jostled each other in the heaving sea. During the transfer to shore, an entire Two Para company got soaking wet when its landing craft inexplicably halted thirty yards short of the beach at San Carlos and an uncaring coxswain ordered the men off into bitterly cold water up to their waists. The condition would prove to be of serious consequence. "Once a man was wet," an officer explained, "he stayed wet. Hanging out clothes to dry is not a recommended practice in forward positions." Especially troublesome were the boots, whose lace holes let water in and whose waterproofing kept it there. In days to come, trench foot, an agonizing ailment brought on by constant damp, would cause more British casualties than Argentine bullets.

Colonel Pike's Three Para was still not ashore when Lieutenant Colonel Jones got his Two Para moving south on a forced march through the dark to its first objective: the 800-foot-high crest of the Sussex Mountains, an east-west ridge between San Carlos and the hamlets of Goose Green and Darwin about sixteen miles farther south, where an Argentine force was known to be garrisoned.

The men soon got a taste of the treacherous Falklands terrain, clambering around huge boulders, tripping over countless smaller rocks, slipping on slimy, mud-laden clumps of tussock grass, sinking ankle-deep into peat bogs, sloshing across an endless succession

Opposed not by Argentine troops but by hilly, barren terrain, the men of Two Para—"laden down like pack mules," in the words of one trooper—slog toward positions on the crest of the Sussex Mountains.

of streams. By the time the column reached the base of the ridge, Two Para had suffered two casualties. One trooper had been knocked unconscious in a fall, and a medic rushing to assist him had fallen into a creek. At dawn, the two were left in the shelter of a gully with a sleeping bag to share, a thermos of hot chocolate, and a supply of signal flares. With the lifting of radio silence later in the day, a medevac helicopter would be summoned for them.

By midmorning, Two Para was digging in atop the Sussex Mountains—and there it would stay for five miserable days.

All the while, Three Para was waiting impatiently to go ashore. By the time the battalion headed for the beach near the settlement of Port San Carlos, sixteen miles across an inlet from where Two Para had landed, daylight was upon them. Some of the men searched the horizon for enemy aircraft, but, as one put it, "at this stage only the gulls, the ducks, and the upland geese were noisily airborne."

The landing itself was uneventful: A contingent of forty-two Argentine soldiers, perhaps awakened from their slumbers by the barking of Falkland Island sheepdogs, promptly fled north. By 11:30 a.m., Port San Carlos and the nearby high ground of Settlement Rocks and Windy Gap were secure. Yet hardly had the troops begun to dig in than the anticipated Argentine air attacks began—and, like Two Para, Three Para settled in for a long, chafing wait while the British fought desperately for control of the air.

To the officers and men of the Parachute Regiment, the very idea of standing around was revolting to every instinct, every aspect of training, every facet of doctrine. By definition, the primary purpose of paratroops is to achieve surprise by materializing behind enemy lines, then to move swiftly toward their objectives and to strike—hard—before their opponents have a chance to react.

In the Falklands, to be sure, both the logistics of distance and the high winds that prevailed there had ruled out any chance of an airborne assault. But most of the men realized that their performance would be judged less by the manner of their arrival than by what they did afterward. "We don't just train for parachuting," said a Two Para corporal. "We train for anything. We know if we're going to have to do it, however we get there, then we're going to do it, just by pushing forward. And that's what we're good at—going forward."

With their cherished red berets now tucked away in their bergens and their winged sleeve patches covered by weatherproof jackets, there seemed little to distinguish the paras from any other foot-slogging soldiers. Except for a company consisting of a reconnaissance platoon and a patrol platoon specially trained for their roles, their battalion organization was identical to that of the regular infantry, with a headquarters company, a heavy-weapons company, and three rifle companies of about 100 men each. Their weapons were likewise conventional—semiautomatic 7.62-mm rifles, general-purpose machine guns of the same caliber, 81-mm mortars, wire-guided Milan antitank missiles, and the usual array of pistols, grenades, and bayonets.

But outward appearances were grossly misleading. Composed entirely of volunteers, the Parachute Regiment subjected its recruits to a grueling twenty-three-week training course that included three months of ground exercises carefully calculated to make a man call upon the last ounce of his physical reserves. "It's not a question of driving somebody until he drops," recalled one para. "It's training him not to drop and to actually go on, and that is what we pride ourselves on. When the time comes for you to pull out that extra fifty or one hundred yards, you can rely on the boys to do it." Only after they had completed that program—and passed a week-long series of physical and mental tests—did the fledglings even begin to learn how to perform the unnatural act of flinging themselves out of airplanes.

The attrition rate was astronomical (about 70 percent failed to qualify), but the graduates were imbued with an extraordinary sense of being somehow invincible. Said Major Chris Keeble, who had spent years in the regular infantry before becoming Two Para's deputy commander: "In an ordinary infantry battalion, there is an undefined limit about what you can do. The philosophy of the Parachute Regiment is that there is nothing you cannot do. There are no limits." A Three Para private in the Falklands put it another way: "As long as he's got wings on his arm, that man is a god."

Such elitist notions are seldom popular, either with other soldiers or among politicians, and over the years the Parachute Regiment had accumulated influential enemies who noted that since World War II the paras had jumped into combat only once—during the 1956 Suez crisis, an occasion most Britons would prefer to forget. Critics argued that the high cost of training and maintaining the paras could not be justified by such earthbound duties as policing Northern Ireland. In 1974, the detractors had forced the disbanding of the Sixteenth Parachute Brigade and in the early 1980s were sharpening their knives for the surviving parachute regiment.

Then came the Falklands crisis—and with it a desperate need for Britain to call on its best. "There was no point in sending the second eleven down there," a Two Para officer said later, speaking in the idiom of cricket. "You had to send the first eleven." That meant the Parachute Regiment, and it was eager to get on with the job.

But first the paras would have to wait and watch helplessly while the air battle raged. Day after day, Argentine pilots in French-made Mirages and U.S.-built A-4 Skyhawk fighter-bombers flashed suicidally low over the Falklands to bomb the British fleet: Time and again, Royal Navy Sea Harrier jump jets and a few RAF GR3 Harriers rose off the flight decks of the carriers *Hermes* and *Invincible* to meet the attackers.

On May 25—a national patriotic holiday in Argentina—the struggle reached a climax: On that dire day, the destroyer *Coventry* and the 13,000-ton container ship *Atlantic Conveyor* were sunk. With *Atlantic Conveyor* went three of the four huge Chinook helicopters with which Three Commando Brigade had planned to airlift both men and supplies in a leapfrogging operation against Stanley. Now, said a brigade officer, "we'll have to bloody well walk."

For Three Para at Port San Carlos, the waiting was relatively tolerable: Most of the men had at least found shelter in the buildings of the little community. But for Two Para on the Sussex Mountains, conditions were wretched. Even at the top of the ridge, the water table lay only a foot or so below the ground's surface, and trenches flooded as fast as the men could bail. To shield themselves from the constant, screaming wind, they huddled within sangars, or walls, hastily built of rocks and chunks of peat. "We were slowly deteriorating," recalled Major Keeble.

No one was in lower spirits than Colonel Jones. Watching the air battle one afternoon, he announced matter-of-factly: "We are not winning. We are losing." Then, the day before the *Atlantic Conveyor* was lost, Jones was further disappointed when part of Two Para started off on a raid against Argentine positions at Darwin-Goose Green—only to be recalled by Brigadier Julian Thompson, the Royal Marine commander to whom the paras had been subordinated. "I've waited twenty years for this," Jones said, furious that a marine was in a position to stop him.

Thompson had little choice. Until the arrival of reinforcements in the form of Five Infantry Brigade, he was under orders to move out of his beachheads only so far as was "safe, sound, and sensible." Clearly, none of those conditions pertained so long as Argentine aircraft were crisscrossing the sky. As it turned out, however, the Argentine Air Force had shot its bolt on May 25. By the end of that day, it had lost forty or more aircraft to Harriers and sheets of antiaircraft fire sent up by British warships. After that, the air attacks virtually ceased, and on the afternoon of May 26, with Five Infantry still at sea, Thompson was summoned to the nearby satellite communications terminal. There, he received peremptory orders to break out of his beachheads. While the main body—marines of 45 Commando and Three Para—was to undertake a long march eastward toward Stanley, Two Para would mount an immediate attack against Darwin-Goose Green.

Thompson protested. The effort at Darwin-Goose Green, he insisted, would only divert badly needed troops from the campaign's true objective at Stanley. He was overruled. Back in Britain, everyone had been stunned by the sinking of five British ships and the loss of sixteen aircraft. The government demanded a victory—now.

At eight o'clock that evening, Two Para set out on the march that would take it to the ferocious little battle of Goose Green and nearby Darwin. The troops traded their heavy bergens for equally burdensome loads of rations, extra ammunition, and spare equipment. The going was slow. Men slipped, slid, and fell, and it was three in the morning before the column reached Camilla Creek house, a long-abandoned farmhouse and

Impulsive and spoiling for action, Lieutenant Colonel Herbert "H" Jones, commander of Two Para, lost his life in a headlong charge against a strong enemy position. Decorated posthumously with the Victoria Cross, Britain's highest award for valor, Jones became a national hero.

outbuildings scarcely eleven miles from Two Para's starting point. Weary, impatient to get out of the whipping wind, the 450 men of Two Para crowded into the residence and two small outbuildings. There, the battalion rested in preparation for a night assault against the outer defenses of an objective about five miles away.

Darwin, which was little more than the property of a sheep company manager, and Goose Green, whose 125 residents made it the Falklands' second-largest community, were situated on an isthmus a mile and a half wide. Within that constricted space, there would be no room for wide-sweeping maneuvers; Two Para would have to punch right through a formidable array of Argentine trenches and gun emplacements.

That was fine with the paras, who were not much given to fancy tactics. Instead, as B Company's commander, Major John Crosland, explained, he and his men would be more than satisfied with "a classic Parachute Regiment punch-up—a gutter fight. Our blokes are bloody good at that, probably the best in the world." In fact, Two Para expected meager opposition: Intelligence had estimated that Darwin and Goose Green were held by no more than an understrength battalion, and it was an article of faith among the British that the hearts of Argentina's conscript soldiers were not really in the fight for the Falklands.

The paras sought to surprise the Argentines by arriving at Darwin-Goose Green sooner than expected. However, that hope was shattered during the afternoon, when men listening to the BBC radio news heard an announcer declare that "a parachute battalion is poised and ready to assault Darwin and Goose Green." H Jones exploded, threatening to bring manslaughter charges against the BBC and anyone else responsible for this blatant breach of security if any of his men were killed because of it. The broadcast ended any chance of swooping down on an inattentive foe—and indeed, the British later learned that Argentine reinforcements were helicoptered into Darwin-Goose Green that evening.

Still, there was no choice but to get on with it, and about four o'clock on the afternoon of May 27, the battalion's officers knelt in a semicircle around Colonel Jones as he explained his battle plan. After dark, Jones said, the paras would move silently toward their start line, which was four and a half miles farther south and just out of sight of the enemy's westernmost positions at Burntside house, a shepherd's abode reported vacant by British scouts. Fire support would be provided by the 4.5-inch gun of the frigate *Arrow* lying offshore; by a mere half-battery of three 105-mm light artillery pieces, all that could be brought to Camilla Creek house that evening by the pitifully few British helicopters; and by two 81-mm mortars that Two Para had been able to lug along the rough track and would carry with them on the assault. These guns would be used when needed to bombard successive layers in the Argentine defenses, which Two Para would then attempt to overwhelm with a series of company-size rushes. Jones's summation required a scant seven words: "Shell them hard, then move in fast."

The plan was the very embodiment of the Parachute Regiment's fighting philosophy. To H Jones, his officers, and their men, war was mayhem, pure and simple. "I don't think people understand the amount of violence that's got to be generated to impress your point of view on somebody who's equally keen to impress his view on you," said B Company's Major Crosland. For added firepower, Two Para, as soon as it got word that it would be going to the Falklands, had scrounged a dozen U.S.-made M79 grenade launchers and increased its complement of machine guns to six.

At about 6 p.m., C Company—the battalion's designated reconnaissance and patrol unit—set off down the trail. Four hours later, A Company, followed by B and D companies, moved through the darkness toward the start line for the attack on Burntside house. Passing behind A Company, B Company continued south, while D Company was held in reserve. At 2:35 a.m., A Company on the British left stormed the house, preceded by antitank rockets fired through windows and doors. Heavy rifle fire was punctuated by exploding grenades. In minutes, the action was over. Thirty Argentine troops observed earlier in a shed near the house had decamped. But contrary to earlier reports, four civilians were inside, flat against the floor. Miraculously, none were injured.

Within three hours, A Company paras had reached their second objective, Coronation Point, separated from Darwin by the mouth of Darwin Bay, a small body of water that opened to the sea on the left. To get to Darwin's small cluster of buildings, the company would have to skirt the water to the right, but that could wait until daylight. "We were all confident that we could have breakfast in the town," one para said later.

Farther to the right, however, B Company was getting all the "gutter fighting" Major Crosland could wish for as it, too, headed toward the bay and Darwin. Bent against a bitter wind and a pelting rain occasionally mixed with snow, attempting without notable success to keep its bearings by compass (at one point, radioed for his position, Crosland replied, "Four hundred yards west of the moon, for all I know."), B Company hammered its way through one line after another of Argentine trenches and machine-gun emplacements. "All this rubbish about them not wanting to fight," said one Two Para officer of the Argentines. "They were fighting hard."

In darkness broken by the lacework of tracer bullets and the blinding glare of high explosives, command and control were impossible to maintain. "Confusion," one officer wryly recalled, "was fairly paramount." Platoons broke down into sections, sections into squads, squads into groups of three or four men until, finally, it was up to individuals to act for themselves. But the troopers of the Parachute Regiment were in their element. "The great quality about our Toms is that they do think," Crosland wrote later. "A lot of people think they're just dozy, hairy-arsed parachute soldiers, all blood and thunder, but they think as well."

Every enemy trench, every bunker, every machine-gun emplacement required a different solution. "You have to adapt to the situation," said a sergeant. "Sometimes you could use fire support to get in there. Sometimes, now and again, we had to use a Milan round on them, hitting the bunker, taking it out, and then charging and taking it. You just get on and do it. It is only afterwards that you think, 'Well, bloody hell.' "

Despite difficulties, B Company made steady progress on a southwesterly course, and by the end of the long night, Two Para seemed in control all along the front. But then came dawn—and a dramatic change in fortunes. As a lieutenant explained, "The light now rapidly appearing enabled the enemy to identify targets and bring down very effective fire." Added Crosland: "Up to first light, we were definitely winning. After first light, it was dawning on people that we were doing the groveling."

Trying to attack an enemy stronghold called Boca house—actually stone ruins—B Company was pinned down by machine guns with long, clear fields of fire. "We just couldn't get across the open ground to get at their machine guns," said Crosland, "and after five hours of fighting, ammunition was critical."

A Company's situation was no better. Moving around Darwin Bay, it had approached a rise in the land, extending from west to east across most of the isthmus, so low and inconspicuous that it had not even been given a map designation. In fact, the Argentine main line of defense had been constructed on this insignificant hummock, which was about to enter history as Darwin Hill.

Swept by a storm of fire from the hill, A Company went to ground, some of the men finding cover at the foot of the slope, others in a gorse gully off to the left. Now, both of Two Para's attacking companies were in trouble.

For officers and men of the Parachute Regiment, trained from their first days to advance aggressively, the situation was a nightmare come true. "The one thing I'd learnt," an officer said, "was to keep the momentum going—if you stopped on a position, you got hammered." Wrote another: "The prerequisite had been to keep the momentum going. That was H's abiding instruction."

Now it was up to the colonel, whose tactical headquarters trailed A Company, to enforce his own instructions. H was understandably testy. When someone proposed a flanking movement, Jones snapped, "Don't tell me how to run my battle." Instead, he joined A Company at the front for a better look at the obstacles ahead. There, an officer suggested that it might be time to call up C and D companies, which had been held in reserve. Jones demurred. "I don't want anyone to come forward until we sort this thing out," he said. "It's a difficult situation."

Indicating an especially well defended Argentine position a short distance away, Jones told A Company's commander, Major Dair Farrar-Hockley, "Dair, you have got to take that ledge." Accompanied by sixteen of his men, Farrar-Hockley rushed at the ledge. Three paras fell dead, and the rest pulled back, hugging the ground for the scant cover it offered. A corporal lying beside Farrar-Hockley told his commander, "Sir, if you don't get out of here now, you aren't going to." It was good advice, but no sooner had Farrar-Hockley and the other survivors crawled away than an officer shouted: "For God's sake come quickly. The colonel's gone round the corner on his own."

Pinpointing another Argentine position, Jones had shouted "Let's go forward." Followed by two noncommissioned officers, he charged, spraying fire from his Sterling submachine gun. Once he went down, but only to change magazines. Then he was back on his feet, charging again—and racing past an Argentine gun pit that he had not seen. "Watch your back!" yelled one of the NCOs.

106

The warning came too late. A machine gun blazed and H Jones was smashed to the ground, mortally wounded at the age of forty-three with a bullet in the back of his neck. Jones was posthumously awarded his country's highest military honor, the Victoria Cross.

Moments later, Major Keeble, 1,500 yards to the rear, received a coded message: "Sunray is down." Command now passed to Keeble—and, thanks to some prudent arrangements, the transition was remarkably smooth. By both tradition and inclination, para commanders lead from the front. To guard against the possibility of a fatal lapse in the event of Jones being killed or wounded, Two Para had established duplicate headquarters, one to accompany Jones and the other, under Keeble, to remain in the rear.

Hurriedly joining A Company at the front, Keeble quickly decided that he needed to find a point "where I could concentrate a large amount of violence in a small sector." His best bet seemed to be on the extreme right, where he had learned that D Company, moving up from reserve, might be able to crawl unobserved along the beach to a position from which it could take the Argentine defenses at Boca house from flank and rear.

The tactic worked, and hardly had the D Company paras started to scramble up a hill toward Boca house than white flags began to flutter from enemy trenches and bunkers. In all, ninety-seven Argentines surrendered.

With the Boca house position broken, the rest of the Darwin defenses became untenable: A Company soon fought its way to the crest of Darwin Hill, and a patrol cleared out Darwin itself. But Goose Green, two miles farther south, remained, and it seemed a certainty that Two Para would have to fight for it. Keeble issued his orders: While A Company, exhausted from its exertions, maintained its grip on Darwin Hill, C Company would push down the middle of the isthmus to approach Goose Green head-on, D Company would advance from Boca house to a position from which it could attack the settlement from the extreme right, and B Company would march down the west coast, then hook inland to cut off Goose Green from behind.

On the map, the plan looked simple. On the ground, it was desperately difficult, and one lieutenant would long remember the "terrifying combination of artillery, mortar, machine-gun, and antiaircraft airburst fire" put up by the Argentine defenders. For the paras, training took over. "Everything you have ever been taught is just second nature," said one. "Those drills are the basis of any attack—they must work."

By nightfall, the paras stood on high ground that dominated Goose Green from the north, south, and west. With its back to water on the east, the settlement was isolated. That evening, Chris Keeble remarked to Major Farrar-Hockley that he might just have somebody "walk down the hill and tell the bloody Argies that the game was up and defeat inevitable. Dair looked at me wearily as if I had lost my marbles."

Keeble did it anyhow. Next day two Argentine prisoners were sent under a flag of truce into Goose Green. Realizing that their situation was hopeless, the Argentines decided to surrender. At 8:30 a.m., an officer in a flashy uniform led 150 men onto an athletic field near Goose Green, made a brief patriotic speech, and ordered them to sing their national anthem. Then, as the Argentines threw down their weapons, Two Para watched in amazement as another 900 soldiers marched out of the village and gave themselves up.

In all, 50 of the enemy had been killed and about 1,200—nearly three times the total number of paratroopers that pressed the assault—were captured. The paras had lost 17 killed and 35 wounded.

On May 27, the same day that Two Para had set off from Camilla Creek house, the battalion-size 45 Commando of the Royal Marines, followed by Three Para, had left the beachhead at Port San Carlos, heading east and slightly south to Teal Inlet, sixteen miles short of Mount Kent and the beginning of the defenses at Stanley. As so frequently occurs with crack outfits, there was an intense rivalry between the Royal Marines and the Parachute Regiment. (The marines called the paras "cherryberries" after their red berets, while the paras hooted at the marines, who wore green berets, as "cabbage heads.") Now, having no intention of bringing up the rear to the marines, Three Para swung out of the long file and took a shortcut to Teal Inlet.

It was an agonizing tramp across the appalling Falklands terrain through torrential rains that shrank the canvas webbing of the men's gear, leaving raw marks on their shoulders. Yet to at least one para there was something reassuringly familiar about the trek. "Somehow," he said later, "one expects 'the real thing' to be different—background music, credits for the cast, something—but

A medic's helmet begins a long line of headgear and other personal equipment laid down in the snow by surrendering Argentine soldiers after the battle of Goose Green. By the end of the twenty-four-day war, more than 11,000 Argentine combatants had been taken prisoner.

there was nothing. It was just like all the training. I found that extremely comforting."

During the epic march, fifteen paras suffered sprained ankles, strained muscles, and similar injuries, and fourteen others were treated for exposure. But to the men of Three Para, the outcome was worth the hardship: Having covered twenty miles in thirty-three hours, they entered Teal Inlet on the evening of May 29. Two nights later, when the marines of 45 Commando straggled into the settlement, they learned that the paras had already pressed on toward Mount Estancia, northernmost of the outer tier of hills that guarded the approaches to Stanley.

That same night, May 31, a company of marines from 42 Commando was airlifted by helicopter onto Mount Kent, not far from Three Para's position on Mount Estancia. The marines were met by special operations troops, who had largely cleared the mountain of Argentine patrols. At 1,500 feet, Mount Kent was the highest of the hills between the British and Stanley, which lay near the eastern end of a fifteen-mile-long peninsula. Wireless Ridge overlooked the town from the northwest, Sapper Hill from the southwest. Between these low prominences and approximately halfway to Stanley lay other hills—Mount Longdon on the left, Two Sisters and Tumbledown Mountain in the middle, and Mount Harriet on the right.

From the summit of Mount Kent, the British could get a good idea of the capital's defenses. They were daunting. The hills ahead bris-

Showing the strain of hard marching and nights out in foul weather, Private Kevin Eaton hunkers down behind his machine gun during a pause in Three Para's trek across East Falkland. Though his unit hoped to catch a much-needed rest, it was ordered to "go firm"—British military jargon for adopting a defensive posture.

tled with 155-mm and 105-mm guns, recoilless rifles, heavy machine guns, and rifle pits—the whole manned by 8,400 men. Fortunately for the British, as it later turned out, much of the Argentine artillery was sited to the east and south, where Menendez had expected the British to attempt amphibious landings.

The early arrivals on Stanley's doorstep would have the better part of two weeks to contemplate these obstacles. By June 5, the rest of 42 Commando had helicoptered to nearby Mount Challenger, and Two Para had advanced unmolested to the settlements of Fitzroy and Bluff Cove on the southern coast. The reinforcing Five Infantry Brigade had expected to be in position to move on Stanley by June 9, after an amphibious landing at Fitzroy and Bluff Cove that began on June 6. But transport and communications difficulties, compounded by an inexperienced staff, dogged the recently organized Fifth. Then on June 8, Argentine Skyhawks sank the landing ship *Sir Galahad* with the loss of fifty-one dead and forty-six injured. Despite these difficulties, Five Infantry was in position to join in the final attack by June 11.

By then, Marine Major General Jeremy Moore had arrived to take overall command of what had become a division-size task force. The plan was for a two-pronged attack on Stanley, with Three Commando Brigade—which now included both battalions of paratroopers—sweeping down from the northwest while Five Infantry pushed up from the southwest. But in the event, Two Para would both see the heaviest fighting and capture Stanley.

Right away, General Moore assigned the Royal Marines of Three Commando Brigade to seize Two Sisters and Mount Harriet—which they accomplished after brisk firefights—and Three Para to assail Mount Longdon, the northern anchor of the enemy defenses.

On the afternoon of June 11, Three Para began a wearying four-hour march to its start line at the base of the 600-foot hill. Arriving shortly after 9:00 p.m., the men listened to last-minute instructions from their officers and NCOs. "Whatever happens," one section leader grimly advised, "keep going, don't stop moving, and if your mate gets hit and he's screaming, leave him alone, don't go near him, or you might get knocked off yourself."

Then, silently, Three Para began to ascend a boulder-strewn hill now bathed in the soft light of a glorious moon.

On the left, A Company met with little opposition as it climbed to the crest of Mount Longdon's northern extremity, where the paras were to establish a firebase. Once there, however, A Company discovered that the position was dominated by higher ground to the south and therefore useless. After an hour and a half, the company was ordered to move partway down the hill and swing south to support B Company, which was engaged in a fight for its life.

Under the command of Major Mike Argue, B Company had begun its ascent of Mount Longdon uneventfully, and the men were making swift progress—until a corporal stepped on an antipersonnel mine that shattered a leg. "That," recalled one officer, "was the end of our silent night attack. For the next eleven hours it was unbelievable nonstop action."

Alerted by the mine's explosion, the Argentine defenders poured down fire from their sod bunkers atop the hill. Almost immediately, the British suffered casualties. "We could see the lads going down," a sergeant remembered. "I thought, 'Oh, my God, this is real.' I'd never seen anything like it before—blokes were being killed, losing limbs, and having their intestines blown out."

As they struggled up the slope, small units became separated and were channeled by enormous boulders into narrow passageways—"bowling alleys," one para called them—down which the Argentines tossed grenades and fired their machine guns and recoilless rifles. All three members of a British Milan missile team were killed by a direct hit from a recoilless rifle. One platoon was reduced from twenty-five men to twelve. When the lieutenant of another platoon was wounded by machine-gun fire, his sergeant, Ian McKay, took command and led four men against the emplacement. One by one, McKay's companions fell, either dead or wounded. But McKay kept on, clearing out the bunker before being killed by a sniper's bullet. Sergeant Ian McKay would also be decorated with the Victoria Cross.

In the maelstrom of their first battle, it was inevitable that various paras reacted differently. Some nearly cracked. Warrant Officer John Weeks came across a platoon commander who was sobbing helplessly. "I gave him a good smack in the mouth because he was hysterical," Weeks recalled. "I said, 'Pick your weapon up and get back and sort your platoon out. They need you.' I'll give him his due; he did bloody well."

Others behaved with a chilling calm. At one point an NCO

watched an eighteen-year-old private whose platoon had been stalled temporarily. Amid the shriek of shells and the whistle of bullets, the youngster had fired up the British soldier's indispensable Hexamine portable cookstove and was making tea while exchanging his wet boots for a dead Argentine's dry ones.

Dawn was near before Mike Argue's B Company had fought its way up to the last Argentine positions, near the summit. B Company had suffered almost 45 percent casualties, with thirteen men killed and twenty-seven wounded, and those troopers still on their feet were exhausted. Colonel Pike, Three Para's commander, ordered A Company to pass through and finish the job—the old-fashioned way: The men charged the enemy trenches with bayonets. Said Pike later, "I shall never forget the sight that morning of

Fresh from a victory at Wireless Ridge, men of Two Para doff helmets and put on their proudest badge of honor—the red beret. One trooper, not realizing that the fighting was over, demurred. "This helmet's staying on until we get on the boat," he said.

A Company advancing through a thick mist with bayonets fixed."

Within another forty-five minutes, the battle for Mount Longdon was ended. Overall, Three Para had lost twenty-three killed and forty-seven wounded, the heaviest British casualties of the war. But fifty Argentines were dead; another fifty had been taken prisoner—and the British were ready to resume their advance toward Stanley.

For the Parachute Regiment, the next objective would be Wireless Ridge—actually two rocky spines extending eastward from Mount Longdon, with a southern spur terminating at Stanley harbor. Clearly, Wireless Ridge would be the last stop on the long, hard road to Stanley, and it was only fitting that Two Para, the victors at Goose Green, would be selected for the task. Though Major Chris Keeble had conducted himself brilliantly in taking over after Lieutenant Colonel Jones's death, London apparently considered Keeble too junior for permanent command and had flown out Lieutenant Colonel David Chaundler to lead the battalion. The caliber of both officers was such that the changeover went without a hitch.

Everyone had learned much from Goose Green. Wireless Ridge would be a far different action from the earlier battle, which had been won on guts alone. Gone were the debilitating shortages of the campaign's first days, and Two Para would have ample fire support for its final battle. Offshore, the frigate *Ambuscade* would hurl in shells from its 4.5-inch gun. Two batteries of 105-mm artillery—a dozen guns—would plaster Argentine positions on Wireless Ridge with 6,000 rounds. In addition to its own mortars, Two Para would have the use of those belonging to Three Para, a total of sixteen tubes. And for mobile firepower, a troop of light tanks—Scimitars with their 30-mm automatic cannons and Scorpions with 76-mm guns—would accompany the paras on their sweep down the ridge.

From the moment of jump-off, forty-five minutes after midnight on Monday, June 14, the operation went better than anyone had dared to imagine. Although occasionally harassed by Argentine artillery and mortar fire, the battalion found enemy trenches mostly abandoned, and the few Argentine soldiers who remained were easily overcome. During the first hours, the closest thing to a British casualty was a para whose boot heel was nicked by shrapnel; diving for cover, he landed in an Argentine latrine.

Still, as Two Para neared the end of the ridge, there was always the possibility that the enemy would brace for a last stand. Instead, as dawn approached, the welcome word was flashed over the battalion's radio network: "The Argies are legging it—they're running everywhere." And at day's first light, Two Para stood looking down across the water at the red roofs of Stanley's 1,000 inhabitants.

With only three men killed, there seemed no reason to stop on Wireless Ridge, and after a hasty conference, Colonel Chaundler ordered Farrar-Hockley's A Company to probe down the road to the Falklands' capital. Just as it was entering town, a small ship sailed across Stanley harbor—bearing on its mast a white flag that signified the Argentine surrender. The war in the Falklands was over.

Three weeks later, when the merchantman *Norland,* en route to the United Kingdom with the paras, put in at Ascension Island, General Sir Edwin Bramall, chief of staff of the British Army, came aboard and delivered a rousing speech of congratulations. When he concluded, one of the paras asked a question: Why had the Parachute Regiment been selected to fight in the Falklands?

"Gentlemen," replied Bramall, "because I wanted to win." ★

Men of Two Para warily enter the debris-strewn streets of Stanley, scarcely able to believe that the war is over. Their caution was well founded; some Argentine commanders, out of touch with their headquarters, did not know that a cease-fire had been arranged and were pondering whether to surrender or to fight on.

Mass Tactical Drop: A Risky Endeavor

Parachuting a large body of troops directly into a battle zone is one of the most hazardous and complex of military operations. Because of the perils involved, it has been attempted under combat conditions only rarely since World War II. Surprise is vital, or the lumbering transport aircraft could be met with devastating ground fire over the drop zone. The paratroopers, jumping into hostile territory—often at night—can easily become disoriented. Obstacles on an unfamiliar drop zone or weather conditions—high winds, for example—can cause injuries among the jumpers and complicate the next phase of the ground mission. Nevertheless, the mass tactical drop retains a place in today's high-tech arenas of combat, and all of the world's major military powers maintain an airdrop-qualified force. The following pages show how the 82d Airborne Division prepares for and executes such an assault.

The objective of a mass tactical drop is to sow confusion among the enemy by knocking out reinforcements, supply lines, and communications channels to front-line units. The drop itself is but one component of a broader offensive strategy: to have ground forces break through the enemy's defenses and link up with the airborne. Until that time, however, the paratroopers are on their own.

Their first task is to secure the drop zone and prepare to meet and repel an enemy attack from any direction. One method used by the 82d is to equip some troopers with portable antitank weapons. These men land close to the edge of the main drop zone, where they swiftly set up antiarmor positions as part of an all-around point defense.

Leaping into enemy territory, a duty fraught with danger and full of unknowns, requires highly motivated soldiers with nerves of steel. That is why a nation's airborne forces are invariably considered the military's elite.

A Lengthy Ritual of Preparation

Outfitting and preparing an airborne unit to jump is an elaborate, time-consuming process. The linchpin is the jumpmaster, an experienced, specially trained paratrooper who has complete responsibility for the men in his charge—regardless of rank—from the prejump briefing to the moment they step out the door. Among his tasks is to thoroughly examine, front to back and head to toe, every harness strap, hook, and connector of each man's main and reserve chutes—plus his combat equipment.

Jumpmasters receive no extra pay; they are motivated by pride and professionalism. Candidates who complete an intensive two-and-a-half-week jumpmaster course, with an attrition rate of 30 percent, gain the added prestige of being looked up to by men who already view themselves as the Army's best. Said one trooper, "When you see a guy walking around with master wings, he's pretty well respected."

Preflight

REPORT TO BRIEFING
The jumpmaster describes the mission, noting the aircraft type, drop altitude, and weather conditions.

DRAW EQUIPMENT
Each trooper collects his main and reserve parachutes. He then teams with a buddy to put on the bulky gear and adjust the numerous straps and buckles.

REPORT TO JUMPMASTER
The jumpmaster makes a rigorous safety check of every trooper.

BOARD THE AIRCRAFT
Under their heavy loads, the troopers shuffle outside to the waiting planes.

A jumpmaster examines a trooper's combat jump rig, which can weigh as much as 150 pounds.

118

The men, loaded with a variety of weapons and equipment, board in "sticks," which are organized according to the tactical priorities of the mission.

Approaching the Moment of Truth

During the flight to the drop zone, the heavily burdened paratroopers sit tightly packed in the aircraft, alone with their thoughts. Having no duties to perform at this point, they are merely cargo. The planes have little soundproofing, so conversation is difficult over the noise of the engines. Some men try to read; others sleep. The Air Force loadmaster, the jumpmaster's counterpart among the flight crew, is responsible for the aircraft's human payload until the plane nears the drop zone.

The navigator announces when the plane is approximately twenty minutes from the drop zone. The jumpmaster rouses his troopers, giving them a few minutes to become fully alert, then begins the prejump checklist, using verbal and hand signals. A few minutes later, a flood of light and a blast of howling wind fill the fuselage as the loadmaster announces, "It's your door, Army!"

Securely braced, the jumpmaster peers out to check the aircraft for obstructions that might snag his jumpers.

With nothing to do and no room to move, paratroopers doze aboard a C-141 en route to the drop zone.

Minutes Out

GET READY
...ch trooper unfastens his ...at belt and observes the jumpmaster.

...BOARD PERSONNEL — STAND UP
...e men with their backs ...inst the plane's fuselage ...ruggle to their feet and ...turn toward the door.

INBOARD PERSONNEL — STAND UP
Those seated back to back along the center of the plane rise.

HOOK UP
The troopers hook static lines—which pull the main chute out of its pack as they jump—to the overhead cable that runs the length of the aircraft. They then gather up the slack in the line, clutching it securely.

Five Minutes Out

CHECK STATIC LINES
Each trooper ensures that the snap hook is correctly attached to the cable. With the help of the man behind him, he traces the line from the cable to his parachute pack for proper routing.

CHECK EQUIPMENT
Everyone inspects his gear again from helmet to boot using one hand, the other still holding the slack in the static line.

SOUND OFF FOR EQUIPMENT CHECK
Starting with the trooper farthest from the door, each signals an OK and taps the man in front of him.

STAND IN THE DOOR
The man nearest the door lets go of his static line. The hook is pushed as far from the door as possible to avoid fouling. The trooper moves to the door and the others shuffle forward.

GO!
As the plane crosses the drop zone, the pilot turns on the green light above the door and the jumpmaster gives the word. The first jumper steps out, followed by the rest at one-second intervals.

At the door, this paratrooper protects the rip cord handle of his reserve parachute as he prepares to step into space.

Hitting the Silk

For paratroopers as well as the aircrews who ferry them, the pass over the drop zone is a perilous interval. Transport aircraft, such as the Lockheed C-141 Starlifter shown here, must fly low, straight, and slow until their payloads of 125 men have all jumped. Any deviation from the straight and narrow—to avoid groundfire, for example—not only raises havoc with the overburdened men trying to make their way to the doors but also risks scattering the jumpers. The consequent delay in re-forming into fighting units on the ground can turn a potentially successful operation into a massacre.

The Trip Down

GOOD BODY POSITION
Exiting the aircraft, the trooper keeps his eyes open, chin down, and elbows in. He bends forward at the waist with feet together and knees locked.

COUNT
As the paratrooper steps through the door, he begins counting by thousands, expecting the jolt of his main chute opening at "four thousand." If no jerk is forthcoming, he deploys his reserve chute.

CHECK CANOPY
The trooper examines his chute for flaws such as blown panels or broken lines that may require using his reserve chute.

Coping with a Multitude of Hazards

Parachutes sometimes fail to perform as expected. A frequent problem is twisted suspension lines. The remedy is a bicycling motion of the legs, which abets the natural tendency of the lines to untwist. More dangerously, the lines sometimes loop over the chute, causing a double or partially deflated canopy. The result is a more rapid descent that increases the risk of injury upon landing and of entangle-ments among jumpers. When a collision is unavoidable, a trooper will spread-eagle and try to bounce off the other chute's suspension lines. In the special case shown above—one trooper has settled onto the parachute of another—air pressure in the canopy allows him to walk to the edge and jump off. He must be quick, however, or the chute below will "steal the wind" of his own and collapse it.

The Final Seconds

KEEP A SHARP LOOKOUT
Approaching the ground, a jumper must be on the lookout for other jumpers and hazards on the drop zone in order to slip away from them.

LOWER EQUIPMENT
At a height of 200 feet or so, the trooper will lower his rucksack on a tether to lessen the jolt of landing.

PREPARE TO LAND
The jumper turns into the wind by pulling on the risers, straps linking parachute to harness. Looking at the horizon, he keeps his legs and feet together, knees slightly bent. As the balls of his feet meet the ground, the trooper collapses onto his side in a smooth, sequential fall, letting his feet, calf, thigh, buttock, then back muscles absorb the shock of impact— about the same as that meted out in a jump from a wall four feet high.

RELEASE PARACHUTE
He releases one riser from his shoulder to spill the air from his canopy. He then hits three quick-release mechanisms on his harness, freeing himself of the parachute that has brought him safely down.

A trooper under a full canopy floats toward impact. Most jump-related injuries occur during landing.

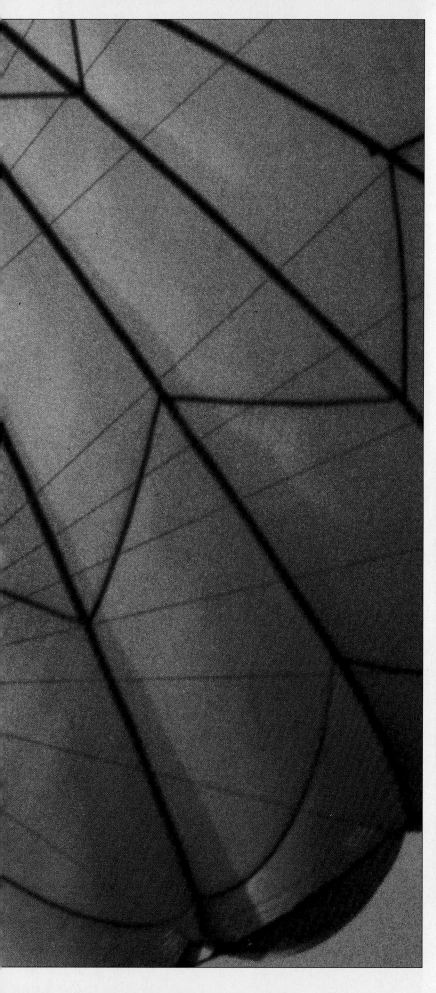

Descent into Battle

After his parachute opens, a paratrooper is well occupied *(box, far left)* during the minute or so that passes before he hits the ground. After he shrugs himself out of his parachute harness, he is ready to rejoin his unit and begin fighting.

To aid in reassembly after a jump, every man has been briefed on the aircraft's flight direction over the drop zone and his unit's assembly point. He can look up and orient himself by watching the departing planes. Then he heads for the rallying point, which is usually marked by colored panels on collapsible poles or lights that are dropped with the unit. The unit commander decides when a sufficient percentage of his strength is assembled to move off the drop zone.

A parachute canopy begins to lose its shape as a trooper's feet hit the ground.

Combat Jump into Panama

Soldiers of the 82d Airborne Division patrol a Panama City street in an M551 Sheridan tank during Operation Just Cause in December 1989. The sandbags covering the lightly armored tank's turret and hull were added for extra protection against rocket-propelled anti-tank grenades.

A flight of eight C-141 Starlifters crossed the night sky over the Gulf of Mexico during the last hours of December 19, 1989, hidden intermittently by soft curtains of cloud. In the belly of each of the giant birds more than a hundred paratroopers of the 82d Airborne Division's ready brigade were crammed together—shoulder against shoulder, knee to knee, cinched into their T-10 Charlies, the U.S. Army's standard-issue, general-purpose parachute. The troopers had a chain of water cups going from large water coolers at either end of the aircraft. Officers were encouraging "prehydration" in readiness for the sweltering heat to come. M60 machine gunner Specialist Vincent Pegues, Third Battalion, 319th Field Artillery, took a few quiet moments for reverie: "I prayed that I'd get out the door, prayed I'd hit the ground, and prayed I'd get to the assembly point," he recalled later.

Nearly a thousand additional troopers of the 82d shivered in their lightweight summer uniforms waiting in C-141s at Pope Air Force Base, adjacent to the home of the division, Fort Bragg, North Carolina. There, planes were slowly being deiced in a freezing rain that would delay the last lift of seven transports for four and a half hours. All were part of a massive airlift of seventy-seven C-141s, twenty-two C-130s, and twelve C-5s that was ferrying not only the entire ready brigade of the 82d but Rangers on their way from Georgia and the state of Washington as well as infantry units based in Louisiana and California. And in the black skies ten minutes ahead of the eight C-141s now en route, thirty-one more Starlifters were toting equipment such as 105-mm howitzers, Humvee all-terrain vehicles, and 39,500-pound Sheridan M551 tanks—all tied down on platforms strapped to parachutes. Nearly 4,000 soldiers strong, this air armada was the largest concentration of airborne might to jump into combat since Korea, and the largest drop for the 82d since World War II, when the division parachuted into Nazi-occupied Holland in August of 1944.

This time the target of the airborne assault was Panama, a nation the size of South Carolina and a friend, home to some 50,000 American civilians. But the friendship had begun to tatter early in 1988 when Panama's military dictator, General Manuel Antonio Noriega, was indicted by two Florida grand juries on charges that he was taking a cut from the drug money being laundered through Panamanian banks. Noriega had simply laughed at the indictments and gone on to wreak havoc on his country's political institutions, dismissing Panama's president in February 1988. After permitting a scheduled free election in May 1989, the dictator cynically prevented the winner, a lawyer named Guillermo Endara, from taking office on October 1. Reacting to these developments, a party of Panamanian Defense Force (PDF) officers marched into Noriega's office on October 3, weapons drawn, and took the dictator prisoner. Loyal PDF units sped to Noriega's aid, captured the renegades, and hauled them off to prison. The ringleaders of the abortive coup were executed by the following day.

In the wake of these events, General Maxwell Thurman, commander of all U.S. troops in Panama, and Lieutenant General Carl Stiner, commander of Fort Bragg's XVIII Airborne Corps, were ordered to revise shelved plans for an invasion, which would later be named Operation Just Cause. Then, with an almost incredible show of bravado, Noriega stood before his rubber-stamp parliament on December 15 and solemnly declared that a state of war existed between Panama and the United States. The next evening, soldiers of the PDF shot and killed a Marine lieutenant and arrested a Navy lieutenant and his wife, witnesses to the shooting. They beat the officer and threatened his wife with sexual abuse. Responding to American outrage at these acts, the PDF went on red alert. President George Bush signed the enabling order for Thurman and Stiner's already well rehearsed blueprint for battle.

"We wanted to go in with a surgical strike on multiple targets, simultaneously," Stiner, tactician of the operation, later explained. "We watched the units that influenced the countercoup," he added. "And then we took a look at the other units that could threaten the safety of civilians."

The core of the PDF was composed of tough, dedicated profes-

128

sionals. Numbering about 3,500 of the 16,000-member armed forces, they included eight light infantry companies and two combat battalions. Of these, the elite Battalion 2000 stood out as having led the rescue of Noriega from the October 3 plotters. All of these troops were well equipped—and not only with weapons obtained from the United States. In recent years, the dictator had been buying Soviet arms from Cuba.

To subdue this force quickly and with minimum casualties on both sides, the generals needed "overwhelming combat power," as Stiner put it, and the troops permanently stationed in Panama would not suffice. There were 13,000 of these soldiers, including some elements of the 82d Airborne that had been brought quietly into Panama during the preceding months, ostensibly for jungle training. To these, the generals would add 9,500 soldiers flown from the United States. About 4,000 of the reinforcements would be special operations troops—the rest would be airborne and light infantry, including the 82d Airborne Division's ready brigade. Combined into six task forces, the nearly 23,000 American soldiers would simultaneously strike twenty-seven carefully chosen targets in or near Panama City and all along the Canal. The operations plan for Just Cause called for all of the objectives to be under American control by daylight on December 20.

When D-day arrived, the ready brigade comprised the First and Second Battalions of the First Brigade and the Fourth Battalion of the Second Brigade. As the plan spelled out, these units would drop onto Torrijos International Airport; the airport was needed in addition to Howard Air Base in Panama. Howard was critical to other aspects of Operation Just Cause, and jumping there would have overloaded the facility. Rangers making a combat parachute assault on the airport an hour earlier at 1:03 a.m.—H-hour was 1:00 a.m. for troops arriving from the United States, 12:45 a.m. for elements already in Panama—would have already secured it as a drop zone and airhead for follow-on elements. Then a fleet of prepositioned helicopters would descend from the skies to taxi the troopers, to be known as Task Force Pacific, to their objectives. Each battalion would hit one of the PDF's key facilities: a barracks in Panama Viejo (the Old City); a hilltop fortress at Tinajitas; and Fort Cimarron, home base of the PDF's Battalion 2000. Two of these garrisons would offer little resistance, while the third would provide the fiercest combat of the war. And after these battles, troopers would plunge into street fighting, rooting out pockets of die-hard Noriega supporters.

Meanwhile, some units of the 82d positioned in Panama before the invasion would join with elements of the Seventh Infantry Division as Task Force Atlantic. They were to secure, among other targets, a major PDF supply depot at Cerro Tigre and the town of Gamboa, where many American families lived. Some of these troops would storm a prison to liberate political prisoners, and yet others would take control of Madden Dam, a strategic water reservoir and hydroelectric plant that supplies electricity for Panama Canal operations, U.S. military installations, and Panama City. Downtown in the capital, a platoon of Sheridan tanks from the 82d's 73d Armor Regiment would aim 152-mm shells at PDF headquarters, the Comandancia, in the first combat the Sheridans had seen since Vietnam. And while the ready brigade was fighting in Panama, another three battalions of the 82d would move to ready status at Fort Bragg, prepared to respond to any other emergency that might arise elsewhere in the world.

Taking the PDF Garrisons

First Lieutenant James Johnson, Second Battalion, First Brigade, was the fourth jumper at the right side door of the Starlifter. Ready to follow him into Panama was his twenty-five-man platoon, a reconnaissance unit whose mission was to set up observation posts for locating and suppressing sniper fire. When he heard the ready order, ten minutes to drop time, Lieutenant Johnson stood up, hooked his static line to the cable overhead, and waited. His rucksack, stuffed with some seventy pounds of gear—M16 rifle magazines, hand grenades, field rations, clothing, a claymore antipersonnel mine, a radio, and extra batteries—hung at his knees. He took heart as he heard Colonel Jack Nix, commander of the 82d's ready brigade, announce that enemy fire on the drop zone was light and wish the troopers "a good jump."

The Starlifter headed into a four-knot breeze and dipped to 500 feet. Johnson glanced at his watch as the jump light turned from red to green: 2:12 a.m. He stepped out the door into the balmy tropical night. As the chute canopied overhead, Johnson saw a fiery spectacle of green and orange tracers arching over the smooth, blacked-

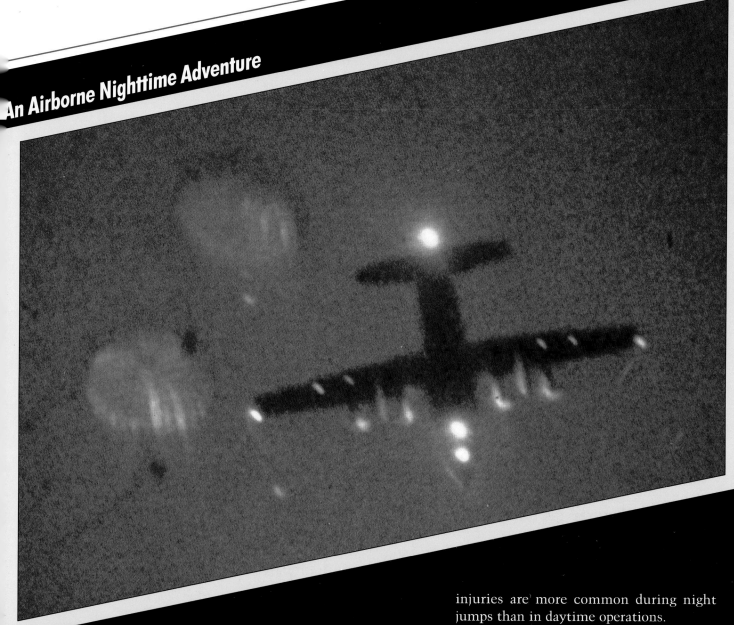

Two 82d Airborne troopers, their parachutes fully inflated, float in the night sky during a training jump from a C-130 transport. The scene was photographed through night-vision equipment.

Parachuting at night can decrease the risk posed by antiaircraft fire and ensure tactical surprise, as it did in Panama. But for the paratrooper, stepping out of a transport plane after dark can be a leap into the unknown, especially if the sky is moonless or overcast. (Night-vision goggles are no help. They severely restrict peripheral vision, so paratroops do not wear them.)

Unless the moon is nearly full, depth perception, for instance, vanishes. Unsure how far he is from the ground, the soldier might lower his 100-pound rucksack too late, increasing the impact of landing. In low light, seeing bushes, trees, and other hazards on the ground is nearly impossible. As a result, injuries are more common during night jumps than in daytime operations.

Even a unit's Sheridan tanks, artillery pieces, and other heavy equipment, air-dropped minutes before the jump, can injure paratroopers who land on them. For this reason, riggers mount small lights atop such gear as they prepare it for airdrop. Troopers following the equipment onto the drop zone can attempt to avoid the tanks and artillery by steering clear of the lights.

Multicolored strobes, flashlights, and chemlights—plastic tubes filled with glowing chemicals—assist the soldiers after they touch down. Used to mark different assembly points, the lights serve as beacons for paratroopers hurrying to rejoin their units and establish a defensive perimeter.

out airfield to his left. Directly under him, he could make out dark shapes. With a shock of recognition, he realized he was over trees. He worried that he might become entangled in branches, be impaled on a limb, or break an arm or a leg—perhaps even hit his head—slamming into a thick bough. Fearful of losing his equipment, he decided not to release the two clips that would lower the rucksack hanging from his waist. His chute hooked onto a large bush, from which he dangled, his toes not quite touching the ground. Shrugging off his parachute, he plopped down.

Most troopers dropped onto equally inhospitable terrain. The area adjoining Torrijos Airport's single long runway had been chosen as the drop zone. The airstrip itself was off-limits because planners did not want it blocked with Sheridan tanks and other vehicles in the early stages of the operation. To a distance of fifty feet or so, the ground alongside was firm and clear of underbrush. Beyond that, elephant grass grew along the edge of a marsh. Farther on, beyond the airport perimeter fence, the terrain was worse—a swamp of streams, swaths of twelve-foot-high elephant grass, groves of trees, and patches of brier. An estimated 40 percent of personnel and equipment landed in this tangle. "In our initial planning, we were determined to keep the runways clear, but I'm not sure that we really considered the impact of the swamp and the tall elephant grass on our ability to rapidly assemble," Major General James Johnson, Jr., commander of the 82d Airborne (and Lieutenant Johnson's father), admitted later.

Sergeant Roy Burgess of the Fourth Battalion, Second Brigade, hit the ground "like a ton of bricks," twisting his ankle. Even so, he was able to jog to his designated assembly area at the northwest corner of the Torrijos runway. He had plenty of company that night among both the injured and the stalwart. Some three dozen troopers sprained or broke knees or ankles in jumping, and like Burgess, many of them refused evacuation.

About a mile and a half from the airport, Captain David Hollands, Third Battalion, 319th Field Artillery, began hacking a path through the elephant grass, encountering soldiers from his battery as he went along. "Sometimes we used our M-9 bayonets," Hollands remembered. "Sometimes it was just a matter of one guy would throw himself down and you'd use the weight of your rucksack and your body to flatten it out." Inching forward in this manner, it took them nearly three hours to reach the airport. Hollands found two of

132

his Humvees and two howitzers on the runway. The other two guns, and the rest of the vehicles, had dropped into the marshes. Unfortunately, the truck that carried the battery's fire-control computer had landed upside down. This handy device took as input the map coordinates and elevation of both an artillery battery and its target. Almost instantly, the machine spit out the direction to point the guns and how high to raise the barrels for a hit. To achieve acceptable accuracy, fire still had to be adjusted according to instructions from a forward observer, but the computer made the process much quicker than the manual tools it supplanted. Fortunately, Hollands had brought along a backup computer, a laptop model that survived the airdrop in working order.

Other airborne units had lost equipment as well, including two of the first eight Sheridan tanks ever dropped into battle. One of the Sheridans was mired up to its turret in a bog; it was wrecked. An engineer crew would blow up the remains to prevent injury from the live ammunition inside it. Another tank had smashed to earth with its parachutes unopened; it was later hauled out and cannibalized for spare parts.

By 4:30, more than two hours later than anticipated, Lieutenant Johnson and other officers were notifying their battalion headquarters by radio that their units were Gavin-4, a code signifying that 90 percent of their personnel had assembled. They were instructed to move to their helicopter pickup points along the Torrijos Airport runway. As they were doing so, the last lift of C-141s carrying members of the ready brigade for Task Force Pacific, delayed four and a half hours by the ice storm in North Carolina, finally discharged its troopers at 5:30 a.m. By that time, the other five task forces of Operation Just Cause either were in the thick of battle, or well on the way to accomplishing their objectives, or in some cases, had already completed their H-hour missions and were awaiting daylight before starting to mop up.

The sun was well up at 7:45 a.m., when at last eighteen UH-60 Black Hawk helicopters arrived, filling the long runway; they would carry the soldiers to their objectives. The scheme called for the Black Hawks to fly in groups of six, thirty seconds apart. Each chopper would ferry twenty troopers. Preceded by scout helicopters and AH-64 Apaches to secure the landing zone, and escorted by AH-1 Cobra gunships, the Black Hawks would shuttle back and forth until every member of Task Force Pacific was deposited in front of his objective. It would take two lifts, estimated at twenty to thirty minutes apart, for the UH-60s to taxi a full battalion. The first lift would organize for the assault—or suppress enemy fire, if necessary—while waiting for the second to arrive.

First priority among the ready brigade's three targets was the barracks built atop the scenic stone ruins of a seventeenth-century town known as Panama Viejo. Situated at the east end of Panama City, overlooking the serene Bay of Panama, Viejo was home to 250 soldiers. Among them were members of Unidad Especial de Seguridad Antiterror (UESAT), Noriega's crack special-operations unit, who had been moved into town from a more remote location after the October coup attempt. Stiner had intelligence that UESAT officers planned to break into five-man teams, go into the city, and take hostages if their fort was attacked.

Lieutenant Johnson, ordered along with others of the Second Battalion, First Brigade, to seize and secure the picturesque, palm-shaded garrison, climbed into a Black Hawk of the first lift and flew west along the coastline. Johnson's reconnaissance platoon was assigned to occupy three observation points near the fort. A sharp-eyed, level-headed young officer, Johnson had trained often for urban warfare. After Panama, he would find these exercises bland.

Johnson's Black Hawk touched down on the tropical beach in front of the garrison, a landing zone code-named Lion. He leaped from the chopper in a hail of automatic AK-47 fire from the barracks, scrambling for cover behind an embankment. About fifteen

Lashed securely to a special air-drop platform, an M551 Sheridan tank starts its descent, yanked from the belly of a C-5 Galaxy by two 28-foot drogue parachutes. Stowed on the platform are eight 100-foot G-11X cargo parachutes that will slow the tank's fall to just over seventeen miles per hour.

134

minutes later, the second group of helicopters hovered a few inches above a deceptively solid-looking shore that was, in fact, a treacherous, oozing stretch of mud flats. Troops sprinted out one side of some of these choppers onto firm ground, while on the other side they sank to their armpits in muck. A few of the choppers lingered for a while, hovering so that soldiers could grab their landing gear and be tugged free. With the tracers still whizzing by, a handful of civilians showing surprising courage formed human chains to pull troopers from the quagmire.

One of the accompanying Cobras sped along the beach, determined to take out a Soviet-made, four-barreled 23-mm ZPU-4 antiaircraft gun perched ominously within range of the hovering Black Hawks. A PDF gunner was scooting over to take his post at the ZPU when he stopped and stared at the approaching menace. The chopper seemed to have the mesmerizing power of its reptilian namesake, and the Cobra gunner could see tremors of fear cross the Panamanian's face. Sizing up his opponent, the PDF soldier made a wise choice. He bolted from the beach. The Cobra's 20-mm Gatling-style cannon demolished the ZPU.

Despite the flurry of fire as Johnson and the others of his battalion landed at the barracks, resistance there turned out to be minimal. Only a few PDF soldiers remained in the buildings by the time U.S. troops appeared, and they fled after a token fight. The others, unknown to the Americans, had been ordered to take up sniping positions in ci- vilian buildings.

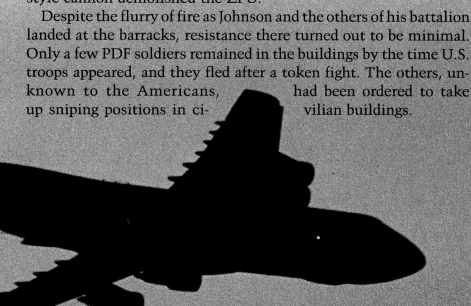

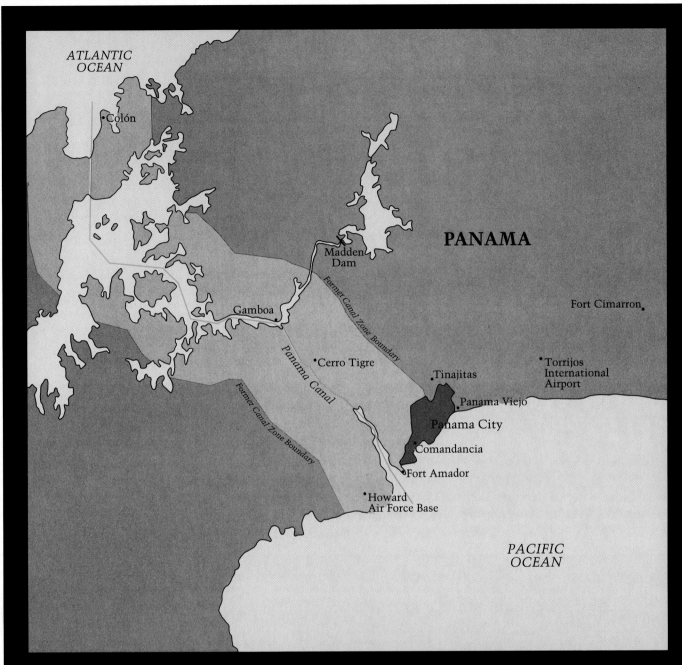

During Operation Just Cause, American forces struck twenty-seven targets. In less than seven hours, paratroopers and other infantry captured Colón, near the Caribbean end of the waterway; rescued political prisoners held at Gamboa, midway between Panama City and Colón; took a logistics center used by the Panamanian Defense Force (PDF) at Cerro Tigre; and secured Madden Dam. Closer to the Pacific, Rangers neutralized two PDF rifle companies at Rio Hato, sixty miles southwest of Panama City, while others jumping northeast of the capital secured Torrijos International Airport. From there, the 82d Airborne assaulted loyalist strongholds at Panama Viejo, Tinajitas, and Fort Cimarron. And in Panama City itself, mechanized infantry stormed the Comandancia, the Presidential Palace, Fort Amador, and lesser PDF facilities.

High-rises were thus proving to be more dangerous than military barracks as, throughout the course of the day, snipers fired down at Americans. Ordinary automobiles were sometimes more deadly than armored vehicles, as PDF troops raced cars through the streets, firing automatic weapons or lobbing grenades from windows as they sped by. A civilian in a sport shirt had to be eyed as warily as a soldier in uniform. As General Stiner would later observe, "Blue jeans had been issued to the Panamanian fighters as a matter of routine so if it got too hot, they could fade back into the city. And that's what they did."

Lieutenant Johnson said he "didn't see a single Panamanian in uniform" all day. He wished his urban combat training had prepared him better for the task of keeping civilians off the street. Sometimes a throng of as many as a hundred would gather. "With all of those people around, you are vulnerable because it just takes one person to come out of that crowd and initiate something," he later recalled. Among those likely to materialize from the crowds with weapons blazing were the men of Noriega's Dignity Battalions—Dingbats as the GIs called them—armed street thugs out for excitement and gain. Just before the previous spring's election, these paramilitary enforcers, at Noriega's behest, had accosted presidential candidate Guillermo Endara and beaten him in the street.

While the war raged in Panama City, American civilians had been under attack at the downtown Marriott hotel off and on since about thirty minutes after H-hour. Masked men had burst into the hotel terrorizing guests and singling out Americans—journalists and business people—to take as hostages, just as Stiner's intelligence reports had predicted. An Eastern Airlines pilot holed up in one of the hotel rooms had been trying to telephone the White House all day to ask for help. Finally he had gotten through and word was passed to Stiner to "do something about the Marriott." The job was turned over to Lieutenant Colonel Harry Axson, who commanded the battalion that had just taken Panama Viejo.

At about 11:00 p.m., Axson dispatched Bravo Company to the Marriott, a few short but murderous blocks from Panama Viejo. Hugging the buildings on either side of the street for the little cover they offered from snipers, two columns of Bravo's troopers sprinted toward their objective; suddenly a large trailer truck rounded a corner onto the dimly lit road. Five members of UESAT wearing black uniforms, protective vests, and balaclavas (similar to the uni-

137

forms of the U.S. Army's Delta Force) blazed away wildly with machine guns from the trailer as the truck barreled between the columns of soldiers, wounding two troopers. Return fire raked the vehicle, setting it on fire, but a passenger inside the cab continued shooting with an automatic pistol, and the truck kept moving.

Specialist James Smith of the Third Platoon happened to be at the other end of the street. Stepping directly into the path of the oncoming truck, he let fly a grenade from the M203 grenade launcher attached to his rifle. His first shot disabled the pistol-firing passenger, and then as the truck came at him, he loaded and fired a second grenade at the driver. The vehicle swerved and crashed into a nearby building. Smith would receive the Bronze Star.

Reaching the hotel, the soldiers encountered little resistance. They found twenty-nine terrified Americans—as well as thirty-five citizens of other countries—who had harrowing tales to recount. Eight men carrying AK-47s had herded about eighty hotel staff and guests into the gilded, chandeliered lobby and forced them to lie facedown on the floor, hands over their heads. "Americans over there!" one man had shouted. He was wearing a red Miller beer T-shirt that proclaimed "American Made."

Eleven American hostages had then been driven to a private home and held in a laundry room where they listened to gunshots, explosions, and the roar of helicopters for three hours. "If a lot of Panamanians have died, we can kill you; don't think we won't," one of their captors warned. At 4:00 a.m., they were shepherded into two vans and, a short time later, released on the street. Some then returned to the Marriott. At 9:00 a.m., a second group of armed men had taken three other hostages from the Marriott who also were to surface later, unharmed. Now, at 11:22 p.m., Company B was gratefully cheered. In appreciation of its arrival, the management brought unlimited free drinks for everyone. The paratroopers, on duty and facing a long night in a combat zone, declined.

Starting after sunup, Task Force Pacific lacked the tactical advantage that General Stiner had considered of paramount importance—the cover of night. The dawn arrival of the last of their number forced their battles into the hours when the PDF would be on the alert and civilians would be jamming the streets. The 82d's unrivaled arsenal of high-tech gadgetry for night operations was useless in the face of what became its most implacable enemy—the brutal tropical sun. Nowhere was the loss of night more costly than for the First Battalion of the First Brigade in the attack on the fortress atop Tinajitas. This easily defended bastion was headquarters for the PDF First Infantry Battalion—Los Tigres, among the best-trained outfits in the PDF.

The landing zone for Tinajitas was on a low ridge about half a mile southwest of the garrison. As the Black Hawk troop carriers approached at about 8:20 a.m., they drew fire from buildings in the adjacent suburb of San Miguelito, reputed to be a neighborhood intensely loyal to Noriega. The PDF had planted 60-mm mortars as well as machine guns atop the fortified hill, and from this vantage point ripped more than ten holes apiece in seventeen of the eighteen helicopters. A Cobra and an Apache both had their gun systems shot out but stayed to help direct the fire from the other escorts.

Having advanced down the ridge to the foot of the garrisoned hill, the troopers began the arduous climb to its summit. The torturous sun struck down more than a dozen soldiers with heat exhaustion. "It was the longest 700 meters I ever did, up that hill in the elephant grass," said Specialist Andrew Slatniske of B Company. Their slow upward crawl throughout the day was punctuated by fire from both the surrounding barrio and the hilltop.

As long as they kept moving, they were able to thwart the onslaught from above, where mortar crews fumbled in adjusting the fall of their shells to each new position of the advancing soldiers. "It could have been very bloody" if the mortar crews had been more competent, Slatniske's platoon sergeant, Joe Sedach, observed. While the towering grass slowed movement, it helped conceal the troopers and reduced the lethal range of shrapnel. For all the fury of the defense, the battalion suffered only twenty-two wounded and two dead: One soldier was killed by small-arms fire as soon as he stepped out of his chopper; another died in a hail of shrapnel from a mortar round. It was 5:00 p.m. before they reached the top of the hill and secured the area. By the time Tinajitas was taken, most of the PDF had disappeared into the nearby village.

Nineteen miles from Tinajitas stood Fort Cimarron, the garrison of Noriega's loyal and disciplined Battalion 2000. U.S. planners feared that these troops might destroy an electrical power station at the fort, cutting off electricity to the city. To prevent such a disruption, the Fourth Battalion of the Second Brigade was assigned to take the post; a mortar platoon from forces prepositioned in Panama conducted an air assault to provide fire support. Battalion 2000 was thought to be such a tough opponent that the Americans decided to bring Humvees and two Sheridan tanks—left at the airport for the other expeditions—along on this one. Thus the assault was delayed until about 5:00 p.m. so that 82d troopers might have the better part of the day to extricate their vehicles from the marshes and clean them up for the drive to the target.

When the 82d arrived at Fort Cimarron, however, the troops found the garrison at quarter strength or less. The preceding night, most of Battalion 2000 had dispersed to the jungle, where they had arms stashed away. Initially, the few soldiers remaining at the fort fought back when the 82d attacked, but after a brief, almost anticlimactic firefight, in which Sheridan tanks loosed eighteen rounds of 152-mm ammunition, the Panamanians stopped firing and melted away. There were no U.S. casualties.

Targets along the Canal

Alpha, Bravo, Charlie, Delta. All four companies of the Third Battalion, First Brigade, had been prepositioned in Panama within recent weeks ostensibly for jungle training. Now they joined with elements of the Seventh Infantry Division into Task Force Atlantic. Its task in Operation Just Cause was to secure a series of objectives along a band that stretched across the isthmus from a point just north of Panama City to the Atlantic Ocean. For Charlie Company, the specific target on this strip of land was Renacer Prison. Situated near the town of Gamboa, the compound contained twenty tin-roofed buildings on a bluff overlooking the Canal. Among the structures were a headquarters building, cellblocks for prisoners, and barracks for guards—all overlooked by several watchtowers.

Noriega had filled Renacer with political prisoners—many from the October coup attempt. Company C's objective was to free these inmates, considered loyal to President-elect Guillermo Endara. There was a danger, however, that prisoners might be injured in the very assault intended to free them, so great care had been taken in rehearsing the mission. In the days preceding the attack, Charlie Company practiced the raid repeatedly in a simulated prison where the locations of cellblocks and even trees were marked with tape.

Teams from Company C also conducted maneuvers at sites near the prison from which they could study the location of fences, construction of buildings, and the competence of the sentries.

Because the prison yard was large enough for only two small UH-1 Huey slicks to discharge troops—fewer than two dozen men and not enough to both rescue the prisoners and tackle the headquarters contingent—a two-pronged attack was planned. The choppers were to deposit soldiers inside the prison to secure the inmates; simultaneously, other members of C Company would land on the banks of the Canal by boat to assault the headquarters. The attack required a precisely choreographed timetable. "If the helicopters landed first, they would have been without support," one of Company C's platoon leaders later explained. "If the boat landed first, it would have tipped our hand." The element of surprise was essential. If the defenders were alerted to the coming attack, they might hold prisoners as hostages. H-hour was set for 1:00 a.m.

As the time for action approached, two OH-58 scout helicopters and one AH-1 Cobra flew along the Canal. One of the scout choppers carried battalion commander Lieutenant Colonel Lynn Moore. Prior to H-hour, the command-and-control scout flew by the prison to see if there were changes to the target that would require modifying plans. The choppers made a second pass to identify the exact positions from which each helicopter would fire. Similar flights, repeated often during the invasion, had lulled the guards into complacency. The two scouts and the Cobra then made a pass at the same moment that the boat and the slicks hit. This time they hovered directly opposite their targets, then opened fire on the watchtowers' guards while using night-vision goggles. This drew the guards' attention away from the prison yard, where the two troop-laden Hueys touched down, door guns blazing. One of the slicks severed a high-tension wire on its way in, causing a blackout, and the Hueys landed in total darkness. The Cobra attack chopper hosed down the guard barracks with its 20-mm cannon. From each of the slicks sprang eleven paratroopers into a fusillade of machine-gun fire from prison guards.

The troopers slipped quickly to the main cellblock, where, a few moments later, as emergency lights switched on, the sound of small-arms fire was lost in the boom of an explosion. An engineer blew the prison door with three pounds of C-4 plastic explosive. Dashing into the building, the soldiers found the prisoners on the

141

Soldiers of the Seventh Infantry Division, braving sniper fire as they hunt for members of Manuel Noriega's paramilitary forces, dash around the corner of an apartment house in Panama City. After the initial assaults, U.S. troops spent most of their time mopping up Panamanian Defense Force holdouts and the so-called Dignity Battalions, often building by building.

floors of their cells, hunched under their mattresses for protection.

Outside the prison compound, meanwhile, the Third Platoon clambered up the bank of the Canal after a two-hour ride in an amphibious landing craft called an LCM-8. There, under intense AK-47 fire from the prison guards, they encountered an obstacle that months of observation had failed to detect—a twelve-foot chain-link fence hidden under the overhang of the headquarters. The platoon waited while two troopers hacked at it with their serrated-edge bayonets as tracers zinged overhead. The wire gave way, and the troopers poured through. They pushed open an un-locked door and entered the darkened headquarters building. They were met with a cloud of tear gas.

Quickly ducking outside, they donned protective masks and re-entered. While his squad pressed the inside attack, Sergeant Kevin Schleben noticed a trail of blood on the floor and followed it outside the building. There he saw two PDF soldiers with their backs to-ward him, crawling in a drainage ditch toward three men in another squad of his platoon. An air-conditioning unit hid the two Pana-manians from the view of the troopers. "I was scared, and at first I didn't do anything," Schleben admitted. Then one of the men reached for his pistol, obviously intending to shoot the three troop-ers. "I thought I'd have problems pulling the trigger," Schleben later recalled, "but when he started to draw his weapon I didn't even think about it." He shot both men. Afterward he would ask the chaplain to say a prayer for himself and the two men he had killed. Schleben was later awarded the Bronze Star.

The firing eventually sputtered out, and by first light the Amer-icans had taken control. Of some forty PDF defenders, five were dead and twenty-two were wounded. The rest had faded into the jungle. Sixty-four prisoners were set free, including two American journalists and the ringleaders of the abortive coup against Noriega. Total U.S. casualties numbered four wounded.

"You must always plan for fear—you can count on it to pervade everything," wrote Lieutenant Clarence Briggs, leader of Bravo Company's Second Platoon, of the part that he played in Operation Just Cause. Briggs remembered barreling along in a CH-47 toward the landing zone for an assault on the Cerro Tigre logistics site. He was clutching his rifle, and his face was awash with sweat. "My gut was in a knot as I watched the intermingling dance of red and green tracers," he recalled after the action. "With knees buckling and heart pounding," he fought to close his mind to the "incessant, paralyzing fear."

The chopper touched down on a golf course adjacent to the supply depot. Briggs and his troopers ran down the ramp at the rear of the helicopter, spread out, and began to crawl through the brush to the fence around the PDF facility. One of the soldiers happened across a hole, and Briggs stood guard while the men of his platoon slipped through, heading for the warehouse on the other side of the fence. A guard, on seeing them, fled.

At the corner of the warehouse, they suddenly found themselves in a cross fire, or so it seemed as bullets zipped past. Almost as one, the entire platoon dropped to the ground. Then Briggs jumped up and raced to a building near the warehouse for a better view of the source of fire. He took some grenades from the ammunition pouch attached to his pistol belt and laid them in front of him. Then he crouched alongside the building and switched his rifle off safe as he spotted soldiers in a road to his front. "I drew a bead and I heard, 'Hurry up and get across the road.' It was a voice from the Third Platoon, assigned to take out the guardhouse" at Cerro Tigre. Their firing had ricocheted across the road to the warehouse, where it narrowly missed Briggs and his men. The lieutenant put his rifle back on safe and breathed a sigh of relief.

Although he was gripped by terror, Lieutenant Briggs had managed to hold his fear in check. Perhaps that very anxiety kept him at the peak of awareness, for Briggs's alertness and cool head had averted one of the most heartbreaking of tragedies in combat—a loss to friendly fire. Others were not quite so lucky as the members of the Third Platoon that Briggs had avoided shooting at and perhaps killing. Bravo Company's only two casualties at Cerro Tigre were the result of shrapnel from American grenades fired from grenade launchers to clear rooms.

Watching the men of his platoon after the battle was over, Briggs observed "the sunken eyes and taut faces. Some were smoking and talking quietly, while others just stared off into nothingness." Even though resistance had been light, he believed that the men were "overwhelmed by the night's events." Later, as he listened to them reconstruct the battle among themselves, he heard echoes of his own "primordial fear."

With sniper fire likely from any quarter, troops were edgy, sometimes feeling endangered by rules of engagement that called for minimum use of force. In such a situation a soldier might find that the line between defending his post and murder can be as thin as the paper on which an indictment is written. First Sergeant Roberto Bryan was to discover this at Madden Dam. Bryan was part of the Third Battalion's Delta Company, which had slipped past PDF roadblocks at H-hour and quickly secured the dam without firing a round or taking a single casualty. The Americans then set up a traffic checkpoint.

Bryan's ordeal began on day three of the invasion when Staff Sergeant Joseph St. John stopped an approaching car that he recognized as one reported stolen by the PDF. He ordered five men out of the car. Inside he found a machete and a tear gas grenade. St. John had the Panamanians spread-eagle on the ground. While he searched them, one stood up, just before a grenade exploded nearby. Later, no one was certain who threw it, but at the time it seemed to most observers that it could only have been one of the five Panamanians. The blast "threw me into the ditch," said St. John, who, along with eight other U.S. soldiers, lay bleeding on the ground, crying out for a medic. In the chaos that followed, other Americans opened fire on the five Panamanians. Four were killed. "Our security forces didn't know if they were going to throw another grenade," explained St. John, who took some shrapnel in the chest. None of the American wounded died.

Bryan jumped out of a command vehicle fifty feet away and rushed toward the checkpoint to survey the wounded. After that, eyewitness accounts differ. One of these witnesses, Lieutenant Brandon Thomas, said he noticed that one of the Panamanians was still moving when Bryan approached and shot the man for no discernible reason. Other witnesses supported Bryan, who said that he saw the man on the ground make a sudden hand motion, ordered him in Spanish to stop moving, and fired his M-16 only after the Panamanian persisted.

Lieutenant Thomas later testified—as did several other witnesses—that he saw Bryan shoot without provocation and use excessive force. Bryan was tried for murder without premeditation, for which the maximum penalty is life imprisonment. In August 1990, after two hours of deliberation, an eight-member court-martial judged Bryan not guilty.

The Comandancia Ablaze

Early in the invasion, as most of the 82d's troops were being taken by helicopter to widely scattered objectives, a platoon of the division's Sheridan tanks was preparing to join elements of the Fifth Infantry Division and the 193d Infantry Brigade to take down a target that General Stiner had his eye on above all others save Noriega himself—the Comandancia, headquarters for the dictator and the PDF. Its capability for command and control had to be destroyed before Stiner could feel the war was going well.

The main edifice in the fifteen-building compound was a reinforced concrete structure with two-foot-thick walls. To assault the heavily fortified compound, Stiner had assembled a powerful force. In addition to the troops on the ground, he had at his disposal two AC-130 Spectre gunships and several Apache helicopters. Each AC-130 boasted infrared gunsights and, among other weapons, a 105-mm howitzer capable of hurling forty-pound projectiles with phenomenal accuracy at targets on the ground; the Apaches would contribute with 30-mm cannons and laser-guided Hellfire missiles.

As the convoy of Sheridans, M113 armored personnel carriers (APCs), and troop trucks was heading toward the Comandancia, it slammed into a wall of fire put up by AK-47s and Soviet-made antitank munitions called rocket-propelled grenades (RPGs), spat from PDF roadblocks improvised from cars, trucks, and cement. Two of the column's APCs were hit by RPGs and exploded. The burning vehicles held up the advance for a half hour. During the pause, a Sheridan provided covering fire while the troops evacuated two killed and eighteen wounded from the wreckage.

The Sheridans and the M113s were able to breach the compound wall with 50-caliber gunfire. The infantry dashed through. The 82d's Sheridans fired 152-mm main-gun rounds into the thick concrete walls of the Comandancia proper and .50-caliber slugs from their cupola-mounted machine guns at the third-floor windows where snipers were blasting away. Two additional Sheridans, pre-positioned on Ancon Hill, overlooking the Comandancia, fired thirteen rounds before smoke and fire blocked visibility. The AC-130, circling lazily in the night sky above the compound, destroyed the third floor of the headquarters building, as well as other targets in the compound. Strafing from above and firing from the Sheridans on

Firelit smoke billowing from the blazing neighborhood of Chorillo silhouettes the skyline of Panama City shortly after H-hour on December 20, 1989. A poor residential area and the site of the Comandancia, Manuel Noriega's heavily fortified headquarters, Chorillo was the scene of some of the heaviest fighting of the entire operation.

the ground eventually set the headquarters building ablaze. An estimated 400 PDF soldiers, dressed in civilian clothes, defended the Comandancia, sniping from within the compound and later moving to buildings outside. A captured PDF soldier reported that by 2:15 all of Noriega's troops had left the Comandancia headquarters building. Eager to secure the prize, U.S. forces cordoned off the compound area. Later in the morning, General Stiner detached a Ranger company from security duty at Torrijos Airport and sent it into the compound to clear the buildings. PDF resistance was light and soon overcome.

In addition to providing cover for PDF troops formerly of the Comandancia, high-rise apartment buildings surrounding the headquarters were home to Dignity Battalion members and their families. From the heights of these sixteen-story buildings, the Dingbats lobbed hand grenades and sprayed the soldiers below with AK-47s and RPGs. U.S. troops shot back with tracer bullets. Incendiary debris from American and Panamanian rounds set ablaze some three square blocks of ramshackle wooden houses in the adjacent poverty-stricken community of Chorillo. Terrified residents poured into the streets. Others were injured and died in their homes.

As the sun burned high over Panama City on the afternoon of the twentieth, most key installations in the downtown area had been subdued. The Comandancia was a charred, ruined hulk, and fires still raged in the surrounding neighborhood. Over the next few days the Americans continued dislodging snipers from rooftops and apartment houses. Roadblocks were disassembled and police guard posts were neutralized.

The citizens of Panama, at first sullen and bewildered, began to salute the Americans with offers of food and soft drinks. They led them to caches of arms stored by the Dignity Battalions. This was perhaps not surprising; the U.S. command was paying a reward for every weapon turned in. Prices ranged from $25 for a hand grenade to $150 for an automatic rifle. Before the campaign was over, it would accumulate some 52,000 weapons of various types.

Major problems remained, to be sure. Thousands of people were homeless in the Chorillo section adjoining the Comandancia. Some

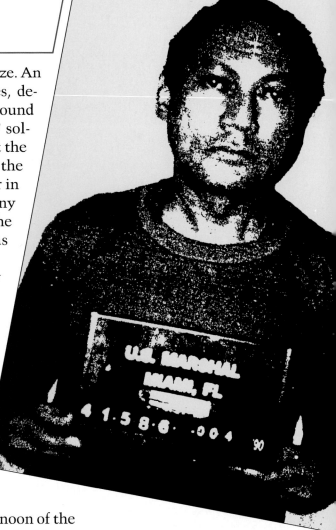

General Manuel Noriega posed for this mug shot, snapped by federal marshals in Florida, two weeks after the invasion. For five days he had eluded capture by scurrying from safe house to safe house; he then sought asylum at the Vatican embassy in Panama City on Christmas Day. Pestered by rock music blaring from loudspeakers ringing the embassy, the weary dictator surrendered nine days later. He was flown immediately to Florida, where marshals arrested him on drug charges.

Panamanians were telling television news crews that men from the Dignity Battalions had deliberately set fires to turn the populace against the Americans. Massive looting had broken out in Panama City, and American MPs were called upon to keep the peace. For help, they enlisted former PDF members—their enemies of hours before now sworn in as allies.

Alliances were also being formed or renewed with former Noriega loyalists. Among these was Captain German Gonzalez Pitti, the captured commander of the fiercely defended Tinajitas fortress. Within a few days of the battle he was returned to his office after swearing an oath to support the new government of Guillermo Endara. Captain Pitti announced his about-face in loyalty with a snippet of homespun philosophizing. The relationship between the Panamanian and American military was like "a marriage engagement; a man can fight and break it off, but it is also possible to kiss and make up," he said.

The fateful hand of war touched the men of the 82d Airborne in unequal measure. Pegues, who had prayed on the flight from Fort Bragg for a successful jump, had his rather modest hopes fulfilled. Burgess—the trooper who twisted his ankle on the airdrop—was riding in a Humvee through the capital on December 22 when he ran into an ambush. The bullets started flying. "My weapon jammed, and I felt something like a softball hit my leg," he reported. "The pain ripped through me." He was taken to Howard Air Base and flown to an Army hospital in Texas.

Captain Hollands, the artilleryman whose computer landed upside down in the mud, carried away vivid impressions of his first war. He remembered a small white car swerving toward him, a passenger inside carrying a grenade. The car accelerated when ordered to stop, and Hollands shot the passenger. "I saw a red spot appear on his head as I fired. Then a bunch of red spots appeared from rounds fired from the other side."

One trooper in Hollands's platoon did not fire his weapon. Instead, when the shooting started, he plucked a small boy from the path of the white car and carried him to safety. No one remembered who the trooper was; he remains an anonymous good Samaritan of the Panama invasion.

Operation Just Cause had its inevitable share of sadnesses, too. One evening, a squad from the 82d's First Brigade was manning a checkpoint when a man started running toward the soldiers with what seemed to be a weapon in his hand. The squad leader fired a warning shot, but the man kept coming, weaving toward them in the darkness. So the squad leader aimed his next shot to wound. He hit the man in the rib cage, killing him. It was all a mistake: The man was a Panamanian civilian on a post-invasion spree, and the object in his hand was a rum bottle.

The many civilian casualties were probably not the result of such misunderstandings so much as the typical fallout of war. Even where there is an effort, as there was in Panama, to keep bloodshed and destruction to a minimum, civilians inevitably pay a price. In Panama, noncombatant deaths were five times as numerous as those among Panamanian military forces and ten times as many as American fatalities. But in absolute numbers, casualties were light on both sides. Twenty-three U.S. soldiers died in the Panama engagement, 4 of them from the 82d Airborne, and 312 others suffered combat wounds or injuries; 79 were 82d paratroopers. On the Panamanian side, there were only about 65 soldiers killed and 124 wounded. Among civilians, the death toll was about 250. More than 1,500 were injured.

Twenty-three days after the war's midnight start, the American soldiers began returning to their peacetime assignments. Noriega had given himself up for trial on drug charges in Florida. The Southern Command gradually resumed the day-to-day chores of garrison duty. And the 82d Airborne flew back to Fort Bragg. It arrived in the best of sky-soldier style—by parachute. ★

After a job well done, Lieutenant General Carl Stiner, ranking paratrooper in Panama, leads men of the 82d Airborne and other elements of XVIII Airborne Corps back to Fort Bragg on January 12, 1990. Following tradition, he and 1,924 soldiers jumped from twenty low-flying C-141 Starlifters, quickly formed up by brigades, and carrying American flags and unit colors, marched in review to the music of John Philip Sousa.

Acknowledgments

The editors of Time-Life Books wish to thank the following for their assistance: Lt. Col. David Abrahamson, Ft. Bragg, N.C.; Julius Alexander, Lockheed Corporation, Marietta, Ga.; Gen. T. G. Allen, Pentagon, Washington, D.C.; Jim Allingham, Aberdeen Proving Grounds, Md.; Diane Andrews, Airborne Forces Museum, Aldershot, England; Nino Arena, Rome; Rex Boggs, Ft. Campbell, Ky.; Maj. Michael Burke, Ft. Bragg; Maj. Nancy Burt, Pentagon; Véronique Cardineau, Paris; Ken Carter, Pentagon; M. Sgt. William D. Childers (Ret.), Oxon Hill, Md.; Francesco Cito, Milan; Christopher R. Colligan, American Helicopter Society, Alexandria, Va.; Shane Cowan, Aldershot, England; S. Sgt. Gordon Darby, Ft. Bragg; Lorna Dodt, Pentagon; Col. Rick Eiserman, Carlisle Barracks, Pa.; Eshel-Dramit, Hod Hasharon, Israel; Capt. John Forrester, Ft. Bragg; Rudi Frey, Rome; Maj. James F. Gebhardt, Travis Air Force Base, Calif.; Capt. Mark Gilette, Inter-American Defense Board, Washington, D.C.; Capt. Barbara Goodno, Pentagon; Richard Groub, Ft. Benning, Ga.; William Harralson, Ft. Campbell; Bill Hayes, Ft. Rucker, Ala.; Lt. Alan Hendricks, Ft. Bragg; Nick Higgins, Campaign Books, Aldershot, England; Hugh Howard, Pentagon; Vadim Ivanenkov, Moscow; Ken Jensen, McDonnell Douglas Helicopter Company, Mesa, Ariz.; Commandant Raymond Jolivet, Second Parachute Regiment, French Foreign Legion, Calvi, France; Brig. Gen. Dennis Kerr, Ft. Bragg; Col. Rick Kiernan, Pentagon; Lt. Col. Myung Kim, Ft. Bragg; Vitali Kolendenkov, Moscow; Aleksandr Kolondarashivli, Moscow; Aleksandr Kurashchin, Moscow; Walt Lang, Pentagon; Elaine Lange, U.S. Congress, Washington, D.C.; Jeff Lindblad, Aberdeen Proving Grounds; Capt. Steve Lindhal, Ft. Bragg; Maj. Gen. Bernard Loeffke, Inter-American Defense Board, Washington, D.C.; Lt. Col. Ken McGraw, Ft. Bragg; Bill Maki, Ft. Campbell; Andrew Mansfield, Aldershot, England; Ercolina Massola, Novosti, Rome; Eric Micheletti, Histoire et Collections, Paris; Joel Miller, Gaithersburg, Md.; Irene Miner, Pentagon; Lyle Minter, Pentagon; Maj. Mike Molosso, Ft. Bragg; Lt. Col. Lynn Moore, Carlisle, Pa.; Foster Morgan, United Technologies, Sikorsky Aircraft, Stratford, Conn.; Col. William Mulvey, Pentagon; Heinz Nowarra, Babenhausen, Germany; S. Sgt. Howell Oliver, Ft. Bragg; Maj. Mike Owens, Ft. Bragg; Col. William Palmer, Fayetteville, N.C.; Sergei Pavlenko, Moscow; Igor Ponomarenko, Moscow; Vyacheslav Puchkov, Moscow; Debbie Reed, Pentagon; Gen. William Roosma, Ft. Bragg; William Rosemund, Pentagon; Gen. William T. Ryder (Ret.), Pinehurst, N.C.; Gene Sexton, Ft. Bragg; Vladimir Shatrov, Moscow; Spanner Spencer, Aldershot, England; Bettie Sprigg, Pentagon; Lt. Col. Gary Steimle, Ft. Bragg; Col. Chuck Steiner, Pentagon; Lt. Col. Jim Swank, Panama City, Republic of Panama; Mabel Thomas, Pentagon; Yuri Tinkov, Moscow; Graham Turbiville, Ft. Leavenworth, Kans.; Mark Urban, London; Ann Wagoner, Stackpole Books, Harrisburg, Pa.; Capt. Mary Jane Wardle, Ft. Bragg; Rep. Charlie Wilson, U.S. Congress, Washington; John Zugschwert, American Helicopter Society, Alexandria, Va.

Bibliography

BOOKS

Aircraft of the United States Air Force. London: Hamlyn Publishing Group, 1987.

Allen, Patrick H. F., *Screaming Eagles: In Action with the 101st Airborne Division (Air Assault).* London: Octopus Publishing Group, 1990.

Anderson, Roy C., *Devils, Not Men: The History of the French Foreign Legion.* Bury St. Edmunds, Suffolk, England: St. Edmundsbury Press, 1987.

Arney, George, *Afghanistan.* London: Octopus Publishing Group, 1990.

Arthur, Max, *Above All, Courage: First-Hand Accounts from the Falklands Front Line.* New York: Viking Penguin, 1985.

Berry, F. Clifton, Jr., *Sky Soldiers: The Illustrated History of the Vietnam War.* New York: Bantam Books, 1987.

Bonds, Ray, editor, *The World's Elite Forces.* New York: Crown Publishers, 1987.

Borovik, Artyom, *The Hidden War: A Russian Journalist's Account of the Soviet War in Afghanistan.* New York: Atlantic Monthly Press, 1990.

Bradley, Col. Francis X., and Lt. Col. H. Glen Wood, *Paratrooper.* Harrisburg, Pa.: Stackpole Books, 1967.

Bridson, Rory, *The Making of a Para.* London: Sidgwick & Jackson, 1989.

Briggs, Clarence E., *Operation Just Cause: Panama, December 1989.* Harrisburg, Pa.: Stackpole Books, 1990.

Carhart, Tom, *Battles and Campaigns in Vietnam.* New York: Crown Publishers, 1984.

Casey, Michael, and the Editors of Boston Publishing Company, *The Army at War* (The Vietnam Experience series). Boston: Boston Publishing Company, 1987.

Cockburn, Andrew, *The Threat: Inside the Soviet Military Machine.* New York: Random House, 1983.

Coleman, J. D., *Pleiku: The Dawn of Helicopter Warfare in Vietnam.* New York: St. Martin's Press, 1988.

Cullen, Tony, and Christopher F. Foss, *Jane's Land-Based Air Defence.* New York: Jane's Publishing, 1989.

Dartford, Mark, editor, *Falklands Armoury.* New York: Sterling Publishing Company, 1985.

Dmytryshyn, Basil, *USSR: A Concise History.* New York: Charles Scribner's Sons, 1984.

Dougan, Clark, and the Editors of Boston Publishing Company, *The American Experience in Vietnam.* Boston: Boston Publishing Company, 1988.

Doyle, Edward, and the Editors of Boston Publishing Company, *America Takes Over* (The Vietnam Experience series). Boston: Boston Publishing Company, 1982.

Dunstan, Simon, *Vietnam Choppers: Helicopters in Battle.* London: Osprey Publishing, 1988.

Dupuy, R. Ernest, and Trevor N. Dupuy, *The Encyclopedia of Military History: From 3500 B.C. to the Present.* New York: Harper & Row, 1986.

Edwards, Roger, *German Airborne Troops 1936-45.* London: Macdonald and Jane's, 1974.

Engle, Eloise, *Parachutes: How They Work.* New York: G. P. Putnam's Sons, 1972.

Eshel, David:
Elite Fighting Units. New York: Arco Publishing, 1984.

The U.S. Rapid Deployment Forces. New York: Arco Publishing, 1985.

The Europa World Year Book 1990 (Vol. 1). Rochester, Kent, England: Europa Publications, 1990.

Fowler, William, *Battle for the Falklands Land Forces* (Vol. 1). London: Osprey Publishing, 1982.

Francillon, René J., *Vietnam: The War in the Air*. New York: Arch Cape Press, 1987.

Frost, Major-General John, *2 Para Falklands: The Battalion at War*. London: Sphere Books, 1983.

Galvin, John R., *Air Assault: The Development of Airmobile Warfare*. New York: Hawthorne Books, 1969.

Geraghty, A. J. V., *March or Die*. New York: Facts on File, 1986.

Gunby, R. A., *Sport Parachuting Handbook: The 1970's Textbook of Sport Parachuting*. Denver: Jeppesen, 1972.

Gunston, Bill:
Modern Fighting Helicopters. New York: Crescent Books, 1986.
Modern Helicopters. New York: Prentice Hall Press, 1990.

Halberstadt, Hans, *Airborne: Assault from the Sky*. Novato, Calif.: Presidio Press, 1988.

Hastings, Max, and Simon Jenkins, *The Battle for the Falklands*. New York: W. W. Norton & Company, 1983.

Hickey, Michael, *Out of the Sky*. New York: Charles Scribner's Sons, 1979.

Hilton, Frank, *The Paras*. London: British Broadcasting Corporation, 1983.

Holmes, Richard, editor, *The World Atlas of Warfare*. New York: Viking Penguin, 1988.

Hoyt, Edwin P., *Airborne: The History of American Parachute Forces*. New York: Stein and Day, 1979.

Isby, David C.:
War in a Distant Country: Afghanistan: Invasion and Resistance. New York: Sterling, 1989.
Weapons and Tactics of the Soviet Army. New York: Jane's Publishing, 1988.

Jones, Kenneth J., *The Enemy Within: Casting Out Demon*. Tortola, British Virgin Islands: Wordsmiths, 1990.

Kesaharu, Imai, editor, *D-Day in Grenada: The 82d Airborne Division in Action*. Tokyo: World Photo Press, no date.

Levy, Alan, *Rowboat to Prague*. New York: Orion Press, 1972.

Mesko, Jim, *Airmobile: The Helicopter War in Vietnam*. Carrollton, Tex.: Squadron/Signal Publications, 1984.

Middlebrook, Martin, *Task Force: The Falklands War, 1982*. New York: Viking Penguin, 1988.

Miller, David, and Christopher F. Foss, *Modern Land Combat*. New York: Crown Publishers, 1987.

Morrocco, John, and the Editors of Boston Publishing Company, *Thunder from Above: Air War, 1941-1968* (The Vietnam Experience series). Boston: Boston Publishing Company, 1984.

Perrett, Bryan, *Weapons of the Falklands Conflict*. New York: Sterling, 1982.

Pimlott, John, *Vietnam: The Decisive Battles*. New York: Macmillan, 1990.

Pimlott, John, editor, *The Elite: Special Forces of the World*. Freeport, N.Y.: Marshall Cavendish Corporation, 1987.

Sheehan, Neil, *A Bright Shining Lie: John Paul Vann and America in Vietnam*. New York: Random House, 1988.

Taylor, Michael, *Encyclopedia of Modern Military Aircraft*. New York: W. H. Smith, 1987.

Thompson, Julian, *No Picnic: 3 Commando Brigade in the South Atlantic: 1982*. London: Leo Cooper, 1985.

Thompson, Leroy:
The All Americans: The 82nd Airborne. New York: Sterling, 1988.
United States Airborne Forces: 1940-1986. New York: Blandford Press, 1986.

Tolson, Lt. Gen. John J., *Airmobility: 1961-1971* (Vietnam Studies series). Washington, D.C.: GPO, 1973.

Urban, Mark, *War in Afghanistan*. New York: St. Martin's Press, 1990.

Walmer, Max, *An Illustrated Guide to Modern Elite Forces*. New York: Arco, 1984.

Watson, Bruce W., and Peter G. Tsouras, editors, *Operation Just Cause: The U.S. Intervention in Panama*. Boulder, Colo.: Westview Press, 1991.

Weeks, John:
The Airborne Soldier. New York: Sterling, 1982.
Assault from the Sky: A History of Airborne Warfare. New York: G. P. Putnam's Sons, 1978.

Windrow, Martin, and Wayne Braby, *French Foreign Legion Paratroops* (Elite series). London: Osprey, 1985.

Young, John Robert, *The French Foreign Legion: The Inside Story of the World-Famous Fighting Force*. London: Thames and Hudson, 1984.

Young, Brig. Peter, *A Dictionary of Battles: 1816-1976*. New York: Mayflower Books, 1977.

Young, Warren, and the Editors of Time-Life Books, *The Helicopters* (The Epic of Flight series). Alexandria, Va.: Time-Life Books, 1982.

PERIODICALS

American Forces Information Service, *Current News: Special Edition*, Nos. 1827-1828. Feb. 1990.

Anderson, Maj. R. B., and Andrew Funk, "Does America Need Airborne Forces?" *Soldier of Fortune*, Mar. 1988.

"Army to Court-Martial Soldier for Shooting Death in Panama." *Washington Post*, July 7, 1990.

Bodansky, Yossef, "Lessons from Afghanistan." *Defence Helicopter World*, Dec. 1989.

Church, George J.:
"The Devil They Knew: How Noriega Was Transformed from CIA Asset to Public Enemy." *Time*, Jan. 15, 1990.
"No Place to Run." *Time*, Jan. 8, 1990.
"Showing Muscle: With the Invasion of Panama, a Bolder—and Riskier—Bush Foreign Policy Emerges." *Time*, Jan. 1, 1990.

Collins, Maj. Joseph J., "The Soviet Military Experience in Afghanistan." *Military Review*, May 1985.

"82d Infantry Division." *Infantry*, Mar./Apr. 1979.

Eshel, Lt. Col. David, "Soviet Airborne Forces." *Defence Update*, May-June 1989.

Fanshaw, Paul, "Target Kolwezi: American SOF Relives Combat Jump with French Foreign Legion." *Soldier of Fortune*, Dec. 1983.

Freedman, Lawrence, "The War of the Falkland Islands, 1982." *Foreign Affairs*, fall 1982.

Friedrich, Otto, "When Tyrants Fall." *Time*, Jan. 8, 1990.

Galloway, Joseph, "Fatal Victory." *U.S. News & World Report*, Oct. 29, 1990.

Gordon, Michael L.:
"Cheney Is Blamed in Muzzling Media." *New York Times*, Mar. 20, 1990.
"Two More G.I.'s Charged with Murder in Panama." *New York Times*, May 6, 1990.

Gung-Ho, Special Issue No. 2, 1984.

Harrison, Lt. Col. Donald F., "Developments in Airmobility in the United States Army." *United States Army Aviation Digest*, June 1969.

Hausenauer, Heike, "The Wounded Come Home." *Soldier*, Feb. 1990.

Hogg, Ian, "Airborne Armoury Soviet Airborne Forces: Weapons and Equipment." *The Elite*, 1986.

Holcomb, Maj. James F., and Graham H. Turbiville: "Soviet Desant Forces." Sept.-Oct. 1988.

"Honours and Awards." *The London Gazette* (Supplement), Oct. 8, 1982.

"Invasion Panama." *Newsweek*, Jan. 1, 1990.

Isby, David C.:
"Afghanistan 1982: The War Continues." *International Defense Review*, Nov. 1982.
"Flying For: SOF Debriefs Four Afghan Hip Pilots." *Soldier of Fortune*, Mar. 1989.

Jenkins, Lt. Col. Jesse F., "A 'Let Down.' " *Flying Safety*, Aug. 1989.

Johnson, Dirk, "Force in Combat: Soldier Tried for Murder." *New York Times*, Aug. 31, 1990.

Kinnard, Lt. Gen. Harry W. O., "A Victory in Ia Drang: The Triumph of a Concept." *Army*, Sept. 1967.

Lacayo, Richard, "Noriega on Ice." *Time*, Jan. 15, 1990.

"The Long Tab, the Long Yomp." *The Falklands War*, Part 9, 1983.

Lopez, Ramon, "US Army Learns Panama Lessons." *Jane's Defence Weekly*, May 12, 1990.

Magnuson, Ed:
"A Guest Who Wore Out His Welcome." *Time*, Jan. 15, 1990.
"Passing the Manhood Test." *Time*, Jan. 8, 1990.
"Sowing Dragon's Teeth." *Time*, Jan. 1, 1990.

Manegold, C. S., et al., "A Standoff in Panama." *Newsweek*, Jan. 8, 1990.

Miles, Donna:
"Panama: Operation Just Cause." *Soldiers*, Feb. 1990.
"Panama: Training to Fight." *Soldiers*, Feb. 1990.
"The Women of Just Cause." *Soldiers*, Mar. 1990.

Miller, Marshall Lee, "Airborne Warfare: A Concept the USSR Actually Can Claim It Invented First." *Armed Forces Journal International*, Oct. 1986.

Moser, Don, "U.S. Paratroopers in a Stepped-Up War: Battle Jump." *Life*, Mar. 10, 1967.

Moyle, Jonathan, "Havoc at Paris." *Defence Helicopter World*, Aug./Sept. 1989.

Nichols, Nick, "Soviet Airborne: Mechanized Strike Force." *International Combat Arms*, May 1989.

"The Night of Battle: Mount Longdon." *The Falklands War*, Part 2, 1983.

O'Ballance, Edgar, "Falkland Islands: The San Carlos Landing." *Marine Corps Gazette*, Oct. 1982.

"The 100-Hour War." *Army Times*, Mar. 11, 1991.

Perrett, Bryan, "Goose Green." *War in Peace*, (London). 1985.

Postlethwaite, Alan, "Red Star Rotors." *Flight International*, Sept. 16, 1989.

Prater, S. Sgt. Phil, "Panama: Combat in the Streets." *Soldiers*, Feb. 1990.

"Putting the Boot On." *The Falklands War*, Part 9, 1983.

Rohter, Larry, "Panama Asks Payments for Arms Seized by U.S. Troops in Invasion." *New York Times*, Mar. 20, 1990.

Rosenthal, Andrew, "General Is in Hiding but His Loyalists Seize at Least 11 Hostages." *New York Times*, Dec. 21, 1989.

Schad, S. Sgt. Dave, "Airborne!: Earning the Wings." *Soldiers*, Apr. 1990.

Schmitt, Eric, "Army Says U.S. Fire Killed 2 G.I.'s in Panama Invasion." *New York Times*, June 19, 1990.

Shortt, Jim, "A Visit to the Soviet Ryazan Higher Airborne Forces Command School." *International Defense Review*, June 1989.

Sider, Don, "In Florida: Jumping with the 82nd." *Time*, July 28, 1980.

Simpson, Ross, "Heroes of Panama: Conspicuous Gallantry for Just Cause." *Soldier of Fortune*, Sept. 1990.

Steele, Dennis, "Operation Just Cause." *Army*, Feb. 1990.

Summers, Col. Harry G., Jr., "Yomping to Port Stanley." *Military Review*, Mar. 1984.

Taylor, Gerri, "Jump Masters." *Soldiers*, Dec. 1987.

Tippy, Margaret G., "Army Women Say, 'Airborne!' " *Soldiers*, Mar. 1989.

Tyler, Patrick E.:
"Army Discloses Second Case of Alleged Murder in Panama." *Washington Post*, May 5, 1990.
"Soldier's Case Raises Issue of Right to Kill." *Washington Post*, July 22, 1990.

"U.S. Paratrooper Acquitted in Killing in Panama Invasion." *Washington Post*, Sept. 1, 1990.

Wilson, George C., "Army Continues Push for More Helicopters." *Aviation Week*, Nov. 30, 1964.

Zaloga, Steven, "Equipment: 'Havoc' at Paris." *Jane's Soviet Intelligence*, Aug. 1989.

OTHER SOURCES

"The Air Assault Division and Brigade Operations Manual." Ft. Campbell, Ky.: 101st Airborne Division, Aug. 1, 1988.

Battery A, 3d Battalion, 319th Field Artillery, "Joint Task Force South in Operation Just Cause: 20 December 1989-12 January 1990." Oral History Interview by Maj. Dennis Levin and S. Sgt. Larry Long. Ft. Bragg, N.C.: Dept. of the Army, Feb. 9, 1990.

"The British Army in the Falklands: 1982." Booklet. Edinburgh: Defence Public Records (DPR), 1983.

"82d Airborne Division Readiness Standing Operating Procedures." Pamphlet. Ft. Bragg, N.C.: U.S. Army, Apr. 1989.

Glantz, Lt. Col. David M., "The Soviet Airborne Experience." Booklet. Ft. Leavenworth, Kans.: U.S. Army Command and General Staff College, Nov. 1984.

Johnson, Maj. Gen. James H., Jr., "Joint Task Force South in Operation Just Cause: 20 December 1989-12 January 1990." Oral History Interview by Dr. Robert K. Wright, Jr. Ft. Bragg, N.C.: Dept. of the Army, Mar. 5, 1990.

Johnson, 1st Lt. James H., III, "Joint Task Force South in Operation Just Cause: 20 December 1989-12 January 1990." Oral History Interview by Dr. Robert K. Wright, Jr. Ft. Bragg, N.C.: Dept. of the Army, June 5, 1990.

"Joint Task Force South: 'Operation Just Cause.' " Booklet. Ft. Bragg, N.C.: XVIII Airborne Corps Public Affairs Office, 1990.

"Implementing the Lessons of the Falklands Campaign." House of Commons Defence Committee Report, Session 1986-87. London: Her Majesty's Stationery Office, May 6, 1987.

"The Laws of War and the Conduct of the Panama Invasion." Report. Washington: Americas Watch, May 1990.

"NBC Operations." Field Manual No. 3-100. Washington: Dept. of the Army, Sept. 17, 1985.

"Operational Summary." Report. Ft. Bragg, N.C.: U.S. Army, no date.

"Operation Just Cause: 82d Airborne Division, 20 Dec. '89-12 Jan. '90." Report. Ft. Bragg, N.C.: U.S. Army, no date.

"Parachute, Personnel Type: 35-Foot Diameter, T-10C Troop Back Parachute Assembly NSN 1670-01-248-9502." Manual. Washington: Dept. of the Army, Sept. 23, 1988.

"Soldiers in Panama: Stories of Operation Just Cause." Pamphlet. Washington: Dept. of the Army, no date.

"Soviet Military Power 1990." Booklet. Washington: GPO, 1990.

Stiner, Lt. Gen. Carl W., "Joint Task Force South in Operation Just Cause: 20 December 1989-12 January 1990." Oral History Interview by Dr. Robert K. Wright, Jr. Ft. Bragg, N.C.: Dept. of the Army, Mar.-June 1990.

"Weapon Systems 1990." Handbook. Washington: Dept. of the Army, Mar. 1, 1990.

Index

102-108; in Falklands, 94-95, *maps 96-97, 98-99,* 101, 102, 111, *113,* 114-115; training, 100; weapons, 100, 104

Great Britain, Royal Army, Third Parachute Battalion: 94-95, 99-101; in Falklands, *92, 94-95, maps 96-97,* 98, 99, 101, 102, 108, *110-111,* 112-114; training, 100; weapons, 100

Great Britain, Royal Marines: Three Commando Brigade, 101, 111; 42 Commando, 110, 111; 45 Commando, 102, 108, 110-111

Great Britain, Royal Navy: ships at Falklands, 101, 111, 114

Grenade launchers: M79, 104; M203, 138

Grenades, rocket-propelled: 147, 150

Guns: 76-mm, 114; 152-mm, 130, 140, 147

Guns, naval: 4.5-inch, 104, 114

Gunships: early, 34

H

Harrier, GR3: 101

Harrier, Sea: 101, 102

Havoc. *See* Mi-28

Helicopters: in Afghanistan, 65, 72, *74,* 75, 76, 77; in Algeria, 34; combat capability, 34-45; development of, 32, 34; in Egypt, *32-33,* 34; extraction of troops, *46-47;* jet, 34; in Korea, 32-33; losses in Vietnam, 57; in Panama, 129, 133-134, 141, 147; roles of, 30-31, 32-33, 37, 40-42, 57; Soviet design, 65, 79; of Soviet VDV, 64; in Vietnam, *28,* 29-31, 42, 44, 45, *46-47,* 48-49, *50-51,* 53, 54, *56-57. See also* individual helicopters

Hellfire missiles: 147

Hermes: 101

Herrick, Henry: 51

Hind. *See* Mi-24

HMMVV (Humvee; Hummer): *20-21,* 127

Ho Chi Minh trails: 43

Hollands, David: 132-133, 151

Howitzers: 105-mm, 20, 22, 40, 43, 53, 111, 114, 127, 133, 147; fire-control computer, 133

Howze, Hamilton: 36, 57

HRS-1: 33

Humvee: in Panama, 127, 133, 140; transport of, *20-21*

Hussein, Saddam: 19

I

Ia Drang Valley: 42, 43

Infantry fighting vehicle. *See* BMD

Invincible: 101

Iraq: army, 20; invasion of Kuwait, 19; prisoners of war, *24-25. See also* Operation Desert Storm

Italy: autogiro, 31

J

Japan: autogiro, 31; and VDV, 62

Johnson, James: 130, 132, 133, 134, 135, 137

Johnson, James, Jr.: 132

Johnson, Lyndon: 42

Johnson, Samuel: 93

Jones, Herbert "H": *95, 96,* 98, *102,* 103, 104, 106-107

Jumpmaster: *118-119, 120,* 121

K

Ka-36/136 (Hokum): 79

Karmal, Babrak: 69

Keeble, Chris: 100, 102, 107, 108, 114

Kinnard, Harry: *37, 41,* 42, 43, 44, 45, 48, 49, 52, 55, 57

Knowlen, Charles: 48

Korea: helicopters in, 32, 39

Kuwait: invasion by Iraq, 19

L

Landing zone. *See* LZ

Larsen, Stanley: 45

Loadmaster: 120

Lodge, Henry Cabot: 55

LZ: 41; extraction from, *46-47;* Spiderweb, 49; X-ray, 49, *50-51,* 52, 53-55, 57

M

M551 (Sheridan) light tank: 20, 22, *126,* 127, 133, 140, 147; airdrop, *134-135;* gun, 130

Machine guns: .50-caliber, 50, 147; 7.62-mm, 53, 64, 100; 12.7-mm, *58;* M60, 127

McKay, Ian: 112

McNamara, Robert: 36, 42

Malvinas. *See* Falkland Islands

Marm, Joe: 53

Marriott hotel, Panama: 137-138

Masoud, Ahmad Shah: 75-76, 77

Medevac: 32, 33

Menendez, Mario: 95, 111

Mi-17 (Hip): 64, *74,* 79

Mi-24 (Hind): *58,* 65, 72, 75; armament, 59, 64; tactics against, 65, 77

Mi-28 (Havoc): *65,* 79

Mi-32: 79

Microlight aircraft: 79

MiG-21: 67, 75

Mines: claymore, 48, 130

Miniguns: .30-caliber, 39

Mirage: Argentine, 101

Missiles, antitank: 64; Milan, 100; TOW, *20-21*

Missiles, laser-guided: Hellfire, 147

Missiles, surface-to-air: in Afghanistan, 76, 77. *See also* Blowpipe; SA-; Stinger

Mobutu Sese Seku: 82, 84

Molosso, Mike: 22

Monroney, Mike: 35

Moore, Harold: 49, 50

Moore, Jeremy: 111

Moore, Lynn: 141

Mortars: aiming, 139; 81-mm, 100, 114; 120-mm, 64

N

Nap-of-the-earth flying: 34

Nix, Jack: 130

Noriega, Manuel Antonio: 128, 140, *150-151,* 152

North Vietnamese Army (NVA): Pleiku campaign, 43-45, 47-49, 52-55, 57

O

OH-13 (Sioux): 45, 47

OH-58D (Kiowa scout): *10-11,* 133, 141

Oliver, John: 47

Operation Desert Shield: *18-19;* and 82d Airborne, 20-22, 24-25

Operation Desert Storm: *4-5;* and 82d Airborne, *24-25*

Operation Just Cause: 128, 136. *See also* Panama

Operation Lam Son 719: 47

Operation Leopard: *80-90*

P

Palmer, Carl: 52

Panama: 128, *map* 136; casualties, 152; Cerro Tigre, 130, *144-145;* Chorillo, *148-149,* 150; civilian deaths in, 152; Comandancia, 130, 147, 150; Dignity Battalions (Dingbats), 137, 142, 150; Fort Cimarron, 129, 139-140; Gamboa, 130, 140; helicopters in, 133, 134-135, 139; Madden Dam, 130, 146; Panama City, 130, 137-138, *142-143,* 147, *148-149,* 150-151; Panama Viejo, 129, 134-135, 137; Renacer Prison, 140-141, 144; Tinajitas, 129, 139; Torrijos International Airport, 129, 130, 132-133; U.S. citizens in, 128; U.S. forces in, 129; U.S. invasion of, 27, *126,* 127-130, 132-135, 137-141, *142-143,* 144-147, *148-149,* 150-151

Panamanian Defense Force (PDF): 128; Battalion 2000, 129, 139, 140; casualties, 152; composition, 128-129; equipment, 129; First Infantry Battalion (Los Tigres), 139; officer coup against Noriega, 128; Unidad Especial de Seguridad Antiterror (UESAT), 134, 137; urban fighting, 137

Parachutes: 122; G-11X, *134;* hazards, *123;* T-10 Charlies, 127

Paratroop assaults: early, 25-26, 60; by Germany, 25-26; limitations, 62; by Soviet Union, 25, 60, 61-62; in Zaire, *80-81,* 82. *See also* Airdrop

Pegues, Vincent: 127, 151

Pennington, Eugene: 48

Pike, Hew: 94, 98, 113

Pitti, Gonzalez: 151

Plastic explosive: C-4, 141

Pleiku campaign: 42-43, *44-45,* 47-49, *50-51,* 52-53, *54-55, 56-57*

R

R-4: 32

Reconnaissance vehicles, amphibious: Soviet, 64

Rifles: AK-47, 138, 144, 147, 150; Lee-Enfield, 72; M16, 130; 7.62-mm, 100

Picture Credits

The sources for the illustrations that appear in this book are listed below. Credits from left to right are separated by semicolons; from top to bottom they are separated by dashes.

Cover: U.S. Army. 2, 3: Sikorsky Aircraft, Stratford, Conn. 4, 5: Bill Gentile/Sipa Press. 6, 7: U.S. Army. 8, 9: Patrick Allen, Bridport, Dorset. 10, 11: Bell Helicopter Textron. 12, 13: McDonnell Douglas Helicopter Company, Mesa, Ariz. 18, 19: Dennis Brack/DOD Pool. 20, 21: Art by Gaylord Welker. 22, 23: U.S. Air Force/M.Sgt. Bill Thompson; Dennis Brack/DOD Pool. 24, 25: 82d Airborne Division, Fort Bragg, N.C., photo by Pete Durban. 28: UPI/Bettmann. 32, 33: Imperial War Museum, London. 37: Charles Bonnay for TIME. 38, 39: Larry Burrows for LIFE—UPI/Bettmann. 40, 41: Courtesy General Harry Kinnard. 44, 45: UPI/Bettmann. 46, 47: National Archives Neg. No. 11C67680. 50, 51: Art by Paul Salmon. 54, 55: AP/Wide World Photos. 56, 57: UPI/Bettmann. 58: Department of Defense. 62, 63: Art by

Stephen R. Wagner; TASS, USSR. 65: C. A. Parlier/ McDonnell Douglas Helicopter Company, Mesa, Ariz. 66: Ullstein Bilderdienst, Berlin. 70, 71: François Lochon/Gamma, Paris. 73: Map by Mapping Specialists. 74: Vladislav Tamarov, USSR. 76: John Gunston/Sipa Press. 78, 79: © Novosti Press Agency, courtesy Soviet Embassy, Washington, D.C. 80, 81: L'Illustration/SYGMA, Paris. 82, 83: Map by Mapping Specialists; Artault/Gamma, Paris. 84, 85: Agence France Presse, Paris—Archives de la Légion Étrangère, Paris. 86, 87: Artault/Gamma, Paris. 88, 89: Berges/SYGMA—L'Illustration/SYGMA, Paris. 90, 91: L'Illustration/SYGMA, Paris. 92-95: Private Collection, London. 96, 97: Maps by Mapping Specialists, designed by Mark Seidler. 98, 99: Peter Holdgate, Plymouth, Devon, England. 102: Topham/The Image Works. 108, 109: Peter Holdgate, Plymouth, Devon, England. 110, 111: Tom Smith/*Daily Express*, London. 113: Airborne Forces Museum, Aldershot, Hampshire. 115: Peter Holdgate, Plymouth, Devon, England. 116-121: Mark Meyer. 122, 123: Antony Platt/Blue Thunder Pictures; Dozier Mobley for UPI/Bettmann. 124, 125: Hans Halberstadt/Arms Communications; David Hathcox/Arms Communications. 126: © Doug Pensinger/*Army Times*. 131: U.S. Air Force/Lem Robson (DF-ST-90-01653). 134, 135: U.S. Air Force/Keith Walker, inset U.S. Air Force/Ken Hammond. 136: Map by Mapping Specialists. 142, 143: Stephen Ferry/Gamma Liaison. 148, 149: Christopher Morris/Black Star. 150, 151: U.S. Marshal Service. 153: Cindy Burnham/*Fayetteville Observer Times*, Fayetteville, N.C.

Time-Life Books is a division of Time Life Inc., a wholly owned subsidiary of
THE TIME INC. BOOK COMPANY

TIME-LIFE BOOKS

MANAGING EDITOR: Thomas H. Flaherty
Director of Editorial Resources: Elise D. Ritter-Clough
Director of Photography and Research:
John Conrad Weiser
Editorial Board: Dale M. Brown, Roberta Conlan, Laura Foreman, Lee Hassig, Jim Hicks, Blaine Marshall, Rita Thievon Mullin, Henry Woodhead

PUBLISHER: Joseph J. Ward

Associate Publisher: Ann M. Mirabito
Editorial Director: Russell B. Adams, Jr.
Marketing Director: Anne Everhart
Director of Design: Louis Klein
Production Manager: Prudence G. Harris
Supervisor of Quality Control: James King

Editorial Operations
Production: Celia Beattie
Library: Louise D. Forstall
Computer Composition: Deborah G. Tait (Manager), Monika D. Thayer, Janet Barnes Syring, Lillian Daniels

Correspondents: Elisabeth Kraemer-Singh (Bonn); Christine Hinze (London); Christina Lieberman (New York); Maria Vincenza Aloisi (Paris); Ann Natanson (Rome). Valuable assistance was also provided by Nihal Tamraz (Cairo); Bing Wong (Hong Kong); Marlin Levin (Jerusalem); Trini Bandrés (Madrid); Elizabeth Brown, Katheryn White (New York); Ann Wise (Rome).

THE NEW FACE OF WAR

SERIES EDITOR: Lee Hassig
Series Administrator: Judith W. Shanks
Art Director: Christopher M. Register

Editorial Staff for *Sky Soldiers*
Picture Editor: Charlotte Marine Fullerton
Text Editors: Charlotte Anker, Paul Mathless
Associate Editors/Research: Robin Currie, Susan M. Klemens, Mark Lazen
Assistant Art Director: Fatima Taylor
Writers: Charles J. Hagner, James M. Lynch
Senior Copy Coordinators: Anthony K. Pordes (principal), Elizabeth Graham
Editorial Assistant: Kathleen S. Walton
Picture Coordinator: David Beard

Special Contributors: Anthony Chiu, Champ Clark, George Constable, George Daniels, Charles W. Sasser, Diane Ullius, Bryce Walker (text); Lois M. Baron, Clay Griffith, Suzanne LaFlair, Sheila K. Lenihan, Anne O. McCarthy, Denise Meringolo, Louis Plummer, Annette Scarpitta, Joann S. Stern, Kathy Wismar, Anne E. Withers (research); Sue Ellen Pratt (art); Mel Ingber (index).

Library of Congress Cataloging in Publication Data
Sky soldiers/by the editors of
Time-Life Books.
　　p.　cm.　(The New face of war series).
　　Includes bibliographical references and index.
　　ISBN 0-8094-8612-1
　　1. Airborne troops. I. Series.
VD480.S59 1991
356'.166—dc20　　　90-21009 CIP
ISBN 0-8094-8613-X (lib. bdg.)

© 1991 Time-Life Books. All rights reserved. No part of this book may be reproduced in any form or by any electronic or mechanical means, including information storage and retrieval devices or systems, without prior written permission from the publisher, except that brief passages may be quoted for reviews.
First printing. Printed in U.S.A.
Published simultaneously in Canada.
School and library distribution by Silver Burdett Company, Morristown, New Jersey 07960.

TIME-LIFE is a trademark of Time Warner Inc. U.S.A.

SEE
10
SANFORD, N. C. 2733(

160